A Kid's Look at Colorado

Phyllis J. Perry

A *Kid's* Look at Colorado

Phyllis J. Perry

Fulcrum Publishing
Golden, CO

Library of Congress Cataloging-in-Publication Data
Perry, Phyllis Jean.
  A kid's look at Colorado / by Phyllis J. Perry.
      p. cm.
  Includes bibliographical references and index.
  ISBN 1-55591-856-5 (pbk.)
  1. Colorado—Juvenile literature. I. Title.
  F776.3.P46 2005
  978.8—dc22

                                        2005023580

ISBN-13: 978-1-55591-856-9

Printed in the United States of America
0 9 8 7 6 5 4 3 2

Editorial: Susan Hill Newton, Faith Marcovecchio
Cover image: Maroon Peaks and Lake near Aspen, Colorado,
  by David L. Perry
Brand designs used courtesy of www.barbwiremuseum.com

Fulcrum Publishing
4690 Table Mountain Drive, Suite 100
Golden, Colorado 80403
800-992-2908 • 303-277-1623
www.fulcrumbooks.com

Dedication

I dedicate this book to all those who enjoy colorful Colorado and offer thanks to the staff at Fulcrum Publishing, who have provided steady support and expertise throughout. I'd also like to give thanks to the many people who have taken their valuable time to write, listen, and talk with me about this project. They have answered questions, loaned books and pamphlets, directed me to sources of data, dug out bits and pieces of information about the fascinating history of Colorado, and offered encouragement when it was needed most. I am especially indebted to C. J. Cassio, Jere DeBacker, Marie Desjardin, Jill Fernandez, David M. Hays, Mary Rose Martorano, Casey J. Miller, Janet M. Miller, Claudia Mills, Ann Nagda, Leslie O'Kane, Sid Weathermon, Celeste Woodley, and Elizabeth Wrenn.

And I offer my deepest appreciation to David L. Perry, whose photographs so beautifully illuminate the text.

Contents

Introduction
A Patchwork Quilt of History

Colorado is a beautiful and fascinating place. Its past and present are filled with tales as varied as the many people who have contributed to the state's colorful story. Each person, place, object, or event is like a tiny swatch of fabric that adds to the overall design of an intricate patchwork quilt of history.

Prehistoric people in Colorado left behind clues of their life stories that scholars now try to interpret from the mysterious ruins of kivas and cliff dwellings. Tales of Native Americans who camped and hunted in Colorado echo in their traditional myths of plants and animals, in the enduring curse of Chief Niwot of the Boulder Valley, and in the indelible memory of the Sand Creek Massacre.

Mesa Verde National Park.

The mysterious legends of the fabled Golden Cities of Cibola and the frightening echoes of ghostly voices surrounding the Purgatoire River remind us of the days of the early Spanish explorers. These were followed by the tales of trappers, traders, and gold seekers who swarmed into the state, later leaving behind a legacy of abandoned mines, ghost towns, and remnants of early forts.

Stories are revealed in diaries recounting the adventures of the brave folk in wagon trains who made their way west through Colorado. Some stayed and joined the ranks of miners, railroaders, lumberjacks, ranchers, and farmers and then eventually brought their families and settled the land. Their tales relate to building train tracks over impossible passes, doing backbreaking work on farms and ranches, and taking part in the rich strikes and terrible busts in the goldfields.

Legendary figures emerge such as Baby Doe Tabor, who died at the Matchless Mine, Silver Heels, who nursed the sick through a smallpox epidemic in Alma, and hardworking burros that toiled underground and came to be known as Rocky Mountain Canaries.

Some of Colorado's beauty has been preserved in parks for people to visit. The crown jewel among these is Rocky Mountain National Park. Connected with this magnificent place are stories of Enos Mills, credited with being the father of the park, Lord Dunraven, who bought up acres of land for a private hunting preserve, and the exploits of fantastic characters such as Isabella Bird and Rocky Mountain Jim.

Countless other Colorado tales relate to the constant struggle to establish towns and cities, schools, and government, and the work involved in building a strong and growing state economy.

Lion Lake No. 2, Rocky Mountain National Park.

In this book, every chapter deals with a segment of the state's past. Woven into each are stories that illuminate that colorful history. Only by piecing together all the tales from all the regions can one finally glimpse the complexity of the whole design that represents the state of Colorado.

Location

Where is this beautiful state? Colorado is close to the center of the western half of the United States. Its northern border is almost halfway between the equator and the North Pole. Six other states are its neighbors—to the west is Utah; Wyoming and Nebraska are to the north; Nebraska and Kansas border Colorado on the east; and Oklahoma and New Mexico are to the south. "Four Corners" in southwestern Colorado is the only place in the United States where four states meet. The four states are Colorado, New Mexico, Arizona, and Utah.

The Rooftop of the Nation

Colorado is noted for its towering mountains. On seeing the amazing view from the top of Pikes Peak in Colorado, Katharine Lee Bates in 1893 wrote her famous song, "America the Beautiful." She describes the spacious Colorado sky, its amber fields of grain, and the majesty of its purple mountains.

The Rocky Mountain region is on the Continental Divide. The divide is a ridge of mountains that runs north and south through the United States. From one side of the divide, waters flow to the west. From the other side of the divide, waters flow to the east. This divide separates the eastern and western slopes of Colorado.

Continental Divide.

Beautiful Colorado is shaped like a rectangle with an area of 103,595 square miles. It is 276 miles from north to south and 387 miles from east to west. Sometimes Colorado is called "The Rooftop of the Nation" because it has the highest average elevation in the United States at 6,800 feet.

But in addition to mountains, there is low land, too. Lush grasslands and many rivers and valleys are found in Colorado. At one point, just east of Holly, the Arkansas River bed is only 3,385 feet above sea level.

Three Parts of Colorado

Colorado can be divided into three main parts: the Great Plains, the Plateau, and the Rocky Mountains. The Great Plains cover about two-thirds of the state's land area. The plains reach from

Kansas and Nebraska across eastern Colorado to the Rocky Mountains. The Plateau region makes up the western part of Colorado, containing mesas, or flat tablelands, as well as valleys along the Colorado and Gunnison Rivers. Near the border of Utah, Colorado becomes dry and desertlike.

The Medicine Bow Range from North Park.

Within the state are 1,143 mountains that are more than 10,000 feet high. More than fifty of Colorado's mountain peaks are taller than 14,000 feet. Mount Elbert, at 14,431 feet, is the tallest mountain in the state. Within this Rocky Mountain region there are four main open areas. Three of these open-grazing areas are called "parks." They are North Park, Middle Park, and South Park. The fourth area, called the San Luis Valley, is the farming section in the southern part of the state.

The San Luis Valley is really a desert. With irrigation, many crops are grown here, but it receives less than eight inches of rain a year. At the eastern edge of this valley are the world's tallest sand dunes, housed in Great Sand Dunes National Park.

A Study in Contrasts

Colorado, with all its parts, is a study in contrasts—green valleys, snow-covered towering peaks, and desert sand dunes, as well as ghost towns and bustling modern cities. Within these pages you will find some of the exciting tales of colorful Colorado that illuminate its rich and fascinating history.

Activities for Further Exploration

1. Make a large outline map of the state of Colorado. Use a separate page for your map legend. On your map legend, list and number each place as you visit or read about it. Put the number of each listing in the correct spot on the map to show where it is located. You might include such things as cities, parks, monuments, mountains, sand dunes, forts, and rivers. You may print out a state map of Colorado by visiting http://www.enchanted learning.com/usa/states/colorado/outline/index.shtml. For a state map showing counties, go to http://www.dola.state.co.us/oem/ cartography/cnty8x112001.jpg.

2. The highest mountain in Colorado is Mount Elbert, which is often called the Top of the Rockies. It is only sixty-one feet lower than Mount Whitney, which is the highest peak in the continental United States. You can see pictures and read an account of climbing Mount Elbert at http://americasroof.com/ co.shtml.

3. Most people have heard of Colorado's mountains, but many do not know that Colorado also has enormous sand dunes. To learn more, read any of these books: *Great Sand Dunes National Park: Between Light and Shadow* by John B. Walker; *The Essential Guide to Great Sand Dunes National Park and Preserve* by Charlie and Diane Winger; or *Great Sand Dunes National Monument: The Shape of the Wind* by Stephen Trimble.

4. In 1893, Katharine Lee Bates looked out at the view from the top of Pikes Peak and wrote a poem that was later set to music and became a popular patriotic song, "America, the Beautiful." Perhaps you'd like to write a poem based on one of your hikes to the top of a mountain or through a forest or along a stream.

Introduction

5

Chapter 1
Colorado's National Parks and Monuments

Colorado is famous for its beautiful national parks and monuments, which are extremely varied. Some are filled with majestic mountains, conifers, and lakes, while others are dry mesa areas. Still others are covered in enormous sand dunes.

Rocky Mountain National Park

Rocky Mountain National Park is one of the wonders of Colorado. Annually more than 3 million visitors from all over the world come to explore it. Many approach through the town of Estes Park.

The first people to settle in Estes Park were Joel Estes and his family. They came in 1860. In 1867, Griffith Evans settled in. Evans opened a modest hotel and rented out cabins to visitors. The following spring, a colorful character named James Nugent moved into the park area. Nugent became known as "Rocky Mountain Jim."

In August 1868, the John Wesley Powell party climbed Longs Peak near Estes Park. In the party was William N. Byers, who was the editor of *The Rocky Mountain News*. Byers wrote a report about the climb and printed it in his newspaper. Soon hunters and mountaineers flooded into Estes Park. So many people came that the Evans family didn't have room for all of them at their house. They built on sleeping porches and rented these to visitors.

In 1872, the Irish Earl of Dunraven came to Estes Park on a hunting trip. He liked the land so much that he wanted to buy it. He thought it would make a great private hunting area. At that time, American citizens could purchase land for $1.25 an acre. The Earl of Dunraven was not a citizen of the United States, so he could not buy land from the government. But he could buy it from citizens who had legally purchased the land, and so he started buying up as many acres as he could.

The very next year, in 1873, having heard about the beauty of the American West, an Englishwoman by the name of Isabella Bird came to visit.

Rocky Mountain Jim and Isabella Bird

No stranger couple is found in the history of Colorado than Rocky Mountain Jim and Lady Isabella Bird. He was a rugged mountain man, and she was an English lady. Together they climbed a towering mountain peak.

Isabella Bird was born in 1831 in Birmingham, England. She was a sickly child, and travel was prescribed by her doctor. That seemed to be all the encouragement Bird needed to begin traveling alone all over the world. She often wrote accounts of her travels, which she sent to her sister. They were eventually published.

In 1873 Isabella Bird's travels brought her to Colorado, where she had a hard time convincing anyone to guide her to Estes Park. She finally succeeded in being led there by two young law students and rented a cabin from Griff Evans. She was overwhelmed by the beauty of the place. Among the spectacular views was one of Longs Peak, a giant of a mountain towering 14,255 feet above sea level. Bird was determined to climb this mountain, which is sometimes called "America's Matterhorn."

To learn more about how to climb the mountain, Bird went in search of Rocky Mountain Jim Nugent, whose cabin was near the entrance of what was later to become Rocky Mountain National Park. In describing his home in *A Lady's Life in the Rocky Mountains*, Isabella Bird wrote that Jim's cabin looked like the "den of a wild beast."

When Jim came out of the cabin to greet her, Bird saw a man of about forty-five years with a striking appearance. One side of his face was handsome. The other side was horribly scarred from his terrible "death hug" encounter with a grizzly bear. One of Jim's eyes was entirely missing.

In earlier years, Rocky Mountain Jim had been a famous scout on the plains. He now lived as a trapper, and his only companion was his hunting dog, Ring. Many people were afraid of this frightening-looking man and considered him dangerous. But by using his best manners and language, Rocky Mountain Jim quickly charmed the visiting English lady.

Although it was thought by some to be too late in the year and far too cold to attempt to climb Longs Peak, Rocky Mountain Jim agreed to lead Isabella Bird and her two young companions up the trail. They left with heavily loaded saddle horses carrying bread, meat, and blankets. Bird wore a pair of borrowed hunting boots.

They rode to "The Lake of the Lilies" and continued onward. The trail became steep, and all the travelers, except for Bird, went on foot. The horses had to stop to rest often. They passed timberline and finally camped at Jim's Grove. There they sat around a huge fire to eat, drink, and finally to sleep.

In the morning, they traveled through the Boulder Field. They scrambled over the rocks and continued on through the Keyhole, a very distinctive notch in the skyline ridge. Then they started walking along the backbone of Longs Peak. This was a very difficult climb, and Jim's dog, afraid of the steep drop-off on either side of the trail, finally refused to go on. He began to howl and sat down to wait for their return.

Bird was not prepared for such a hard climb either, and Jim had to half carry her up the steep ascent. They abandoned one approach because it was too icy. But they found another. The last bit of the climb, though only 500 feet, was so steep that they slowed to a crawl, and it took them an hour. They triumphantly placed their names on a sheet of paper kept in a tin wedged in a crevice at the very top, indicating they had successfully made the climb. Without staying long, they began their descent.

The two young men went back one way, while

Rocky Mountain Jim led Bird down another trail that he thought would be easier for her. She was exhausted, but Jim helped her at every step, carrying her when necessary. Back at the spot where they had left their horses, Bird was lifted up on hers and lifted down again when they finally reached their campground.

They spent another night before going down the rest of the way in the morning. Bird didn't sleep that night, but listened to the stories told by Rocky Mountain Jim. Bird wrote that she would not exchange her experience in climbing Longs Peak with its memories of "perfect beauty and extraordinary sublimity for any other experience of mountaineering in any part of the world."

Isabella Bird.
Courtesy of Tom Noel Collection

After a long visit, Isabella Bird left Colorado and Rocky Mountain Jim remained. By 1874, the Earl of Dunraven had bought about 15,000 acres of land in the area. He put up fences and tried to keep other settlers out. Rocky Mountain Jim owned a critical piece of property at the entrance to the area, and he would not sell his land to the earl.

There were many disputes between homesteaders and the Earl of Dunraven, who still wanted to set up his own private hunting preserve. Some men, like Griff Evans, who made his living caring for tourists, liked the hunting preserve idea. Others, like Rocky Mountain Jim, did not. This disagreement was probably the reason that Evans shot and killed Rocky Mountain Jim one day as Jim was riding past Evans's cabin. There are several differing accounts of this shooting. No one knows for sure what happened, but Evans was never charged with a crime.

The Earl of Dunraven hired a man named Whyte to take care of his property. Whyte found he simply couldn't keep people off the land. He finally gave up and left in 1896. Three men eventually bought the Earl of Dunraven's land. They were named Enos A. Mills, Freelan Oscar Stanley, and J. D. Sanborn, of Greeley.

Enos Mills is called the father of Rocky Mountain National Park. Mills studied the plants and animals of the area. You can still visit his homestead cabin, which was placed on the National Register of Historic Places in 1973.

Enos Mills's homestead.

Mills was a small man who stood only five feet, five inches tall and weighed about 125 pounds. But he stands like a giant in the history of the park. He wrote seventeen books and hundreds of articles about this beautiful part of the country. And he made more than 2,000 speeches describing its beauties.

Mills knew the park very well. He personally guided 257 ascents up Longs Peak. He explored in winter as an official snow observer and measured the snow depth along the Continental Divide. Largely due to the work of Enos Mills, a law was passed in 1915 that set aside the land that became Rocky Mountain National Park.

F. O. Stanley, the Stanley Steamer, and the Stanley Hotel

Freelan Oscar Stanley was a very important figure in the growth of the town of Estes Park. He and his twin brother, Francis Edgar Stanley, were born in Kingfield, Maine, a long way from the rugged mountains of Colorado.

The two brothers were very ingenious. Between them they invented the first X-ray machine, the dry plate photographic process, and an automobile known as the Stanley Steamer.

After making a fortune by selling the dry plate photographic process to Eastman Kodak, the brothers enjoyed designing and manufacturing cars. They raced and set speed records with their steam cars. In 1898, a world speed record of twenty-seven miles per hour was set by a Stanley Steamer in Watertown, Massachusetts. The twins gained a lot of publicity when they drove a Stanley Steamer to the top of 6,293-foot Mount Washington in New Hampshire in 1899 and even more publicity when one of their cars gave a president of the United States his first ride.

When he was fifty-three, F. O. Stanley contracted tuberculosis and was given only one year to live. So in 1903, Stanley brought his wife to the high, clean air of Estes Park, Colorado. He helped to develop the town of Estes Park by promoting electricity, sewage service, medical care, and banking.

He designed and then built the beautiful Stanley Hotel in Estes Park, which is still in operation today. The hotel was finished in 1909, complete with its own power plant, manor house, casino, tennis courts, nine-hole golf course, trap shooting range, and airfield to accommodate small planes. It was the first all-electric hotel ever built in the United States. It cost a half a million dollars to build at that time, and Stanley paid for everything in cash.

More and more tourists wanted to visit the area.

Many people would take the train from the Northeast to Lyons or Loveland, Colorado. Then a fleet of thirteen Stanley Steamers would transport the passengers to Estes Park where guests stayed at the Stanley Hotel. The hotel is currently designated a National Historic Landmark.

Along with the hotel, Stanley thrived in Estes Park. He lived in the area until he died at the age of ninety-one. In his last few years, he experimented with making violins.

The Stanley Hotel, Estes Park.

The little town of Estes Park has grown to about 5,500 people and still serves as the gateway to Rocky Mountain National Park. The park preserves the land and the animals that live there. Some people think it is the greatest treasure in Colorado.

The park contains 226,324 acres. Some of the people who visit the park travel along Trail Ridge Road, which is the highest continuous highway in the United States. This road crosses the Continental Divide at Milner Pass. At its highest point, the road reaches 12,183 feet above sea level.

The highest point in the park is Longs Peak. It is 14,255 feet high. Major John Wesley Powell and his party first climbed this peak in 1868. Although Isabella Bird's climb with Rocky Mountain Jim was made famous in her writings, the first woman to climb the peak was Addie Alexander in August 1873. Soon after, Anna Dickinson became the second woman to climb Longs Peak.

There are fifteen routes to the summit. Fewer than 2,000 people have climbed the east face. It is 1,500 feet of vertical rock.

Longs Peak, Rocky Mountain National Park.

Agnes Vaille

Agnes W. Vaille was a Colorado mountaineer determined to climb the east face of Longs Peak in winter. After three unsuccessful attempts, she persuaded Walter Kiener, a recent immigrant from Switzerland, to accompany her. On January 12, 1925, during blizzard conditions, she realized her goal and reached the summit.

Agnes Vaille.

While descending, Vaille and Kiener reached the Boulder Field and Vaille fell, exhausted and unable to continue. She had been climbing for twenty-five hours in temperatures far below zero.

Her climbing partner went to summon help and met a search party at timberline. But by the time the rescuers arrived, Agnes Vaille was dead from exposure. One of the members of the rescue team also became lost and died of exposure. Kiener lost some toes and fingertips to frostbite, but he recovered. Later he became a Longs Peak climbing guide.

Rocky Mountain National Park has more than 300 miles of hiking trails. Many short trails are close to roads and campgrounds. Some can be traveled on horseback. Backpackers travel to more-remote areas. They sign up for permits that allow people to hike and camp in the more isolated parts of the park.

Many plants, birds, and animals live in the park. Bighorn sheep, American elk, mule deer, black bears, coyotes, bobcats, martens, and cougars call the park home. There are also marmots, chipmunks, ground squirrels, and pika. Among the birds are grouse, owls, woodpeckers, jays, nuthatches, chickadees, and juncos. Above treeline are pipits, rosy finches, horned larks, and ptarmigan. More than 750 kinds of plants are found in the park.

The park is a favorite spot in the fall. People come to see the golden aspen leaves and the majestic elk. Huge bull elk and their herds of females come down to the meadow areas each evening. Visitors park their cars and watch the elk grazing in Horseshoe Meadow. Sometimes a young bull elk wanders too close to the herd of another bull. Then one bull elk will chase the other away. The bull elk makes a strange bugling sound, like a high-pitched squeal, to call his herd together.

Mesa Verde National Park

Mesa Verde National Park covers more than 52,000 acres of land. It is located in Colorado near the towns of Cortez and Mancos. It became a national park on June 29, 1906, and was made a World Cultural Heritage Site in 1978. This park contains thousands of archaeological sites including the best-preserved cliff dwellings in the United States. The remains at these sites offer clues about the Ancestral Puebloans, or "Ancient Ones."

People lived in Mesa Verde from about A.D. 550 through A.D. 1300. First they lived in pit houses. These houses were in small villages on the mesa tops. People got their food by hunting, gathering, and farming. Later they built houses aboveground using poles and adobe construction. Finally, they built stone houses. And about A.D. 1200 they began living in cliff dwellings. It is for the cliff dwellings, built into crevasses in the cliffs like small apartments, that the area is now famous.

Visitors can look at cliff houses and rooms called kivas. *Kiva* is a Hopi Indian word for "ceremonial room." It may also have been used as a workroom and a gathering place. Entry to a kiva is by ladder. Down in the kiva there is a fire pit in the center of the floor. A kiva usually has six pillars that support the roof. There is also a recessed area on the south side of the kiva, although no one knows exactly how this area was used.

Some kivas have a small hole in the floor between the fire pit and the wall. This is called a *sipapu*, or "spirit hole." It is an entrance into the underworld.

Around A.D. 1300, the Ancestral Puebloans left their homes. They probably moved to New Mexico and Arizona. Their reasons for leaving Mesa Verde are not clear. Possible reasons are lack of rain and attacks from other Native American tribes.

Cliff Palace, Mesa Verde National Park.

Great Sand Dunes National Park

The Great Sand Dunes of Colorado are located in the San Luis Valley. They cover an area about seven by five miles. The Rio Grande River and its branches helped form the dunes from sand deposits. Westerly winds blow over the San Juan Mountains. The winds pick up sand and deposit it at the east edge of the valley. Then the air rises again to cross the Sangre de Cristo Mountains.

Medano Creek is a small stream that begins in the Sangre de Cristos. It is fed by melting snow. In spring and early summer, it flows along the eastern edge of the dunes. The water from the stream ripples along the sand. Finally it disappears belowground.

Great Sand Dunes National Park.

The Great Sand Dunes became a national monument on March 17, 1932. On September 13, 2004, the Great Sand Dunes was upgraded to a national park. These massive dunes are located near Mosca, Colorado. The new park contains about 107,000 acres of forests, grasslands, wetlands, alpine lakes, and tundra and has six peaks taller than 13,000 feet.

Black Canyon of the Gunnison National Park

Black Canyon of the Gunnison National Park is located near Montrose, Colorado. It was made a national monument in 1933. It became a national park on October 21, 1999. The landscape in the area was formed over a period of 30 million years. Water cut through rock to form the deep, fifty-three-mile-long gorge. Some of the sheer canyon walls drop as much as 2,700 feet.

John W. Gunnison was a graduate of West Point Academy. He traveled in the West working as an army engineer. In the Salt

Black Canyon of the Gunnison National Park.

Lake area, he mediated between settlers and Native Americans during an uprising.

In May 1853, John Gunnison led an expedition to survey a Pacific railroad route. He led his party across the Rocky Mountains through Cochetopa Pass by way of the present Gunnison and Green Rivers to the Sevier River. He camped near the Sevier River in Utah Territory and was killed there on October 26, 1853, by Pahvant Indians in revenge for an earlier attack upon their people by a party of white emigrants headed for California.

Many hikers visit the area today. They can explore the North Rim, South Rim, and inner canyon routes. Among favorite spots are the Painted Wall, Chasm View, and Pulpit Rock.

Colorado National Monument

Colorado National Monument was established on May 24, 1911. The monument contains 20,453 acres, including canyons and tall pieces of red sandstone. Bighorn sheep, golden eagles, mule deer, and mountain lions live there.

Many visitors take the Rim Rock Drive. This is a twenty-three-mile paved road. It goes from the Colorado River Valley to the top of the Uncompahgre Plateau. The drive goes from 4,700 to more than 7,000 feet. Viewpoints provide a look at its many special features, including layers of rock from various formations.

Rock climbers enjoy climbing the spires and cliffs. They especially like to scale the Wingate and Kayenta Formations. The most popular climb is Independence Monument, which stands 350 feet high. John Otto was the first to climb it. Otto later worked hard to get this area made into a national monument.

Dinosaur National Monument

Dinosaur National Monument is located near Dinosaur, Colorado, and Vernal, Utah. Long ago, this area was a low-lying plain crossed by rivers and streams. It was home to many dinosaurs. Living there were *Apatosaurus, Diplodocus, Stegosaurus*, and *Allosaurus*.

Floodwaters washed lots of dinosaur bones onto a sandbar. More sediment piled on top of these bones. Over time, the riverbed turned into hard sandstone and mineralized the bones buried within it. Much later, rain, frost, and wind wore away layers of rock and exposed the fossil treasures.

Earl Douglass was a paleontologist from the Carnegie Museum in Pittsburgh, Pennsylvania. He explored this area in 1909. On top of one of the ledges he found the tailbones of an *Apatosaurus*. The site became a national monument in 1915. Visitors can see many fossil bones in their natural setting here. The dinosaur quarry is surrounded by canyon country. The canyons of the Green and Yampa Rivers were added to the original park in 1938.

Florissant Fossil Beds National Monument

Florissant Fossil Beds is in a mountain valley just west of Pikes Peak. Almost 35 million years ago, volcanoes erupted in this area. Ash buried the valley and its trees. Eruptions continued to occur for 5,000 to 10,000 years. Eventually a lake formed. Insects and plants were caught in sediment at the bottom of the lake. They were pressed into layers of shale and preserved as fossils.

On August 20, 1969, the area was set aside as a national monument. Paleontologists collect fossils from there, and the specimens are sent to museums all over the world. Most of the fossils are of plants and insects, but fossil remains of an ancient horse and of piglike animals have also been found.

Hovenweep National Monument

Hovenweep National Monument is located near Cortez. It is made up of six units of ruins on 784 acres. The ruins are prehistoric sites of farming villages. The people who lived there were similar to the people of Mesa Verde.

These ancient people of Hovenweep started farming in the San Juan area about 2,000 years ago. At first they lived in caves. Then they built pit houses in valleys and on mesa tops. Finally they built surface houses in rows. They raised corn, beans, and squash, hunted, and trapped animals. They also made tools and jewelry.

These people moved to the Hovenweep canyons by A.D. 1200. They got their water from permanent springs in this area. Using stone, they built houses and towers. The towers had lookout spots. From here they could see the approach of friends or enemies. Some of the stone walls and twenty-foot-tall towers remain. These ancient people left before A.D. 1300. Lack of rain may have been the reason they left.

There are many animals in the area including deer, coyotes, foxes, and bats. There are also ravens and hawks. Visitors may use a campground and hike a number of different trails.

Garden of the Gods Park

Garden of the Gods is a park located in a valley near the base of Pikes Peak west of Colorado Springs and a little north of Manitou Springs. This is not a flower garden. It is a garden of spectacular rocks. Its colorful rock formations have names such as Balanced Rock, Kissing Camels, and Indian Head. Rufus Cable was one of two surveyors who explored the area in 1859. He called it a place that was fit for the gods.

The red color of the rock formations is due to ferric iron. The Rocky Mountains began to rise about 60 million years ago. At that time, the area, now known as Garden of the Gods, tilted skyward. Wind

Garden of the Gods, Colorado Springs.

and rains carved the special rock shapes over a long time.

In 1871, General William Jackson Palmer founded Colorado Springs. He did this while extending the lines of his Denver and Rio Grande Railroad. His friend was Charles Perkins, president of the Chicago Burlington & Quincy Railroad. Palmer urged Perkins to build a summer home in the area. Perkins did not build a home, but in 1879 he did buy land in Garden of the Gods. After his death in 1907, his family gave the land to the city of Colorado Springs for a park.

Activities for Further Exploration

1. It takes many people a lot of time and work to create and maintain our national parks, so we should not take them for granted. You might want to learn more about the history of our parks. If so, a helpful resource is *Our National Park System: Caring for America's Greatest Natural and Historic Treasures* by Dwight F. Rettie. To see an alphabetical listing of our national parks, their sizes, locations, and major features, see http://www.infoplease.com/ipa/A0884500.html.

2. Many people believe that Rocky Mountain National Park is one of the most beautiful of all our national parks. If you are going to visit the park, check in advance at http://www.rocky.mountain.national-park.com/cal.htm for a calendar and list of activities. You might want to participate in the Junior Ranger Program. Children's Adventure is a ranger-led program for kids 6–12 with many hands-on activities about geology and wildlife. For example, in Skins & Skulls, you will learn about moose, elk, bighorn sheep, bobcats, and other creatures that live in the park.

3. Dinosaur National Monument is a popular spot. To learn more about it, you might write a letter requesting information. Include a nine-by-twelve-inch stamped, self-addressed envelope so that a pamphlet and other materials might be mailed back. The address is Visitor Information Headquarters, Dinosaur National Monument, 4545 E. Highway 40, Dinosaur, Colorado 81610-9724. You can also read about the monument on the Internet at http://www.nps.gov/dino/.

4. Try drawing a picture of one of your favorite scenes of a Colorado national park or monument. You might use chalk, magic markers, watercolors, or crayons. Many park headquarters post student pictures in the visitor headquarters or put them on the Internet for others to enjoy, so that if you wish, you can share your vision of a national park or monument with others.

Chapter 2
Historic Sites and Ghost Towns

Present-day Colorado is filled with reminders of its past. There arc dilapidated buildings from towns that once boasted busy gold, silver, and coal mines. There are pieces of roundhouses, tunnels, and railroad tracks. There are traces of early forts, trading centers, farms, and ranches.

Many of these historic sites are marked. Sometimes extensive ruins of these abandoned places remain. Old ghost towns are favorite trip destinations of Coloradans and tourists alike.

Bent's Fort

At one time, Santa Fe, New Mexico, belonged to Mexico and before that to Spain. Many people from the United States went to Santa Fe to trade. Mountain men and Native Americans would bring in beaver pelts and other furs, and they would trade these for blankets, knives, traps, and beads.

Outside of Bent's Fort.

25

William Bent and Bent's Fort

William Bent was born in 1809 in St. Louis, Missouri. He was one of four sons of a Missouri Supreme Court justice. But Bent was not headed toward a career in law. He was interested in the outdoors and in fur trapping and trading.

By the age of fifteen, Bent was trapping along the upper Arkansas River in Colorado. In 1829, he journeyed with his brother, Charles, taking a wagon train of trade goods to Santa Fe. Charles sold the goods he brought with him and then returned to the East.

Charles Bent continued to come back and forth to Santa Fe to trade over the years. He became a famous merchant. Years later, his good business sense was recognized when Charles Bent was chosen to serve as governor of New Mexico.

Unlike his brother, William Bent did not return to St. Louis. He liked this new country and decided to stay and live in the mountains. He trapped beaver and traded with the Native Americans. He would go to Santa Fe to buy supplies such as beads and knives. He would take these by packhorse into the Native American villages where he would trade his goods for their furs and buffalo robes.

Bent was good at trading, but he knew it would be easier if he did not have to carry so many supplies with him. He thought the Native Americans would come to a fort to trade their furs. Bent talked over his plans with his brother, Charles. They chose a spot on the north bank of the Arkansas River in American territory for their fort, and they formed a partnership with Ceran St. Vrain. They built the fort in 1833. There they bought and sold manufactured goods, horses, mules, Mexican blankets, buffalo robes, and all kinds of pelts.

William Bent married a Cheyenne Indian called Owl Woman in 1835. She was the daughter of Chief Gray

Thunder. Together they raised four children. After Owl Woman died of smallpox, Bent followed the Native American tradition of marrying her sister, Yellow Woman.

When war with Mexico broke out in 1846, Bent guided General Phil Kearney's troops along the Santa Fe Trail into Mexico. He also supplied the troops from his trading post. The government did not pay him for his goods and services and tried to buy his trading post for a very small price.

William Bent.

Some say that William Bent, angry at the murder of his brother in Taos during an uprising and angry at the actions of the government, deliberately blew up the fort. Others say the explosion was the accidental result of a fire. Whichever was the case, Bent built a new outpost about thirty-eight miles downstream from Old Bent's Fort. With a group of settlers, he founded a colony there. It was first called Fort William and later was known as Fort Lyon.

In 1859, the Pikes Peak gold rush brought many more people into the area. Bent tried hard to keep the peace between whites and the Cheyenne, but he failed. There were many battles, including the Sand Creek Massacre.

William Bent died of pneumonia in 1869 and was buried in Las Animas, Colorado.

Old Bent's Fort was an interesting structure. It was 180 feet by 135 feet. Trees were scarce in this country, so the fort was built out of adobe bricks. The walls were fifteen feet high and four feet thick at the base. There were sturdy plank doors to the fort. It had two round lookout towers with cannons and small holes for shooting rifles. Sleeping and living rooms, a storage house, and a corral were inside the walls of the fort.

When it was finished, it was the largest trading fort in the Southwest. As many as 100 people sometimes lived in the fort. A well in the courtyard supplied some of their water. Each day, someone took a wagon with barrels to the river to bring back more water. Hunters went out from the fort to kill game for meat. Kit Carson was one of these early hunters. He often worked at Bent's Fort.

Sometimes mountain men would spend the winter inside the fort. They passed long evenings talking. There were few books in the western country, and many of the men could not read. But sometimes on long winter evenings, a man would read to the others in the fort. Favorite readings came from the Bible and the plays of William Shakespeare.

In the spring, wagons traveled from Bent's Fort to Missouri carrying buffalo robes, beaver pelts, and other animal hides. These were sold, and more trading goods were bought with the money.

Many people wrote about Old Bent's Fort in letters and diaries. Some drew sketches of it. These were all helpful when the destroyed fort was reconstructed in 1976. It is now a well-visited tourist spot.

Fort Vasquez

Fort Vasquez was another important trading center for Native Americans. It was located between Fort Laramie to the north and Bent's Fort to the south. This was a good location on the South Platte River. It was near what is now Platteville, Colorado. Native Americans brought hides and furs to the fort, which they traded for blankets, kettles, and other goods.

This adobe fort was built in 1835 by fur traders Louis Vasquez and Andrew Sublette who worked for the Rocky Mountain

Fort Vasquez plaque

Fur Company and had a license to trade with the Cheyenne and Arapaho Indians. When the demand for beaver pelts dropped, the owners sold the fort in 1841. Native Americans destroyed it in 1842.

The building fell into ruins, but some of the walls remain. Parts of the site have been excavated. There is now a museum store and visitor information center where visitors can learn what it was like to be an early fur trader. Fort Vasquez is listed in the National Register of Historic Places.

Sand Creek

The Sand Creek Massacre occurred on November 29, 1864. At this time, Native Americans were unhappy with white settlers. These settlers were not simply passing through; they planned to stay and farm and ranch. The Native Americans did not welcome them for fear of losing their hunting grounds to these new settlers. The Native Americans raided homesteads, burned ranches, and attacked wagon trains.

A meeting with several tribal chiefs took place on September 28, 1864. The Native Americans were told to report to a fort and surrender. Some Native Americans came into the fort, but Chief Black Kettle did not. Black Kettle came back again, not to surrender, but to discuss peace. He was sent away.

Before any more peace talks took place, Colonel Chivington, who led the Civil War troops from the Colorado Territory, arrived. He and his men were told about the Native Americans camped nearby who had not come in to surrender at the fort. Most of

29

Colonel Chivington's men had signed up for only 100 days of army service. They were not well trained nor well disciplined.

Colonel Chivington used his 750 Colorado volunteers to attack the Native American village where Chief Black Kettle was staying. Also in the village were lodges belonging to the Southern Cheyenne and Arapaho. The camp was along the bed of Big Sandy Creek in southeastern Colorado.

Chivington's men attacked the village at four in the morning. The Native Americans were taken by surprise and many were killed. Some say sixty-nine Native Americans died. Other reports suggest several hundred were killed, including women and children. Colonel Chivington's troops suffered fifty-four casualties including those killed and wounded.

The United States Army and Congress held investigations to find out exactly what had happened at Sand Creek. The people who testified told different stories. No one was punished for taking part in the massacre. Colonel Chivington retired from the army in 1865. Black Kettle, who survived the attack at Sand Creek, was killed at another battle in Oklahoma in 1868.

On November 7, 2000, President Clinton signed into law the Sand Creek Massacre National Historic Site Establishment Act. It authorizes the National Park Service to deal with private landowners to buy the needed land. Then this land will be marked and recognized as a historic place. During the summer of 2005, President Bush signed further legislation transferring title of the land from the tribes to the National Park Service.

Ludlow

Ludlow is now a ghost town, but at one time it was a busy coal mining community. On September 23, 1913, 9,000 miners stopped working in the mines and went on strike against the Colorado Fuel and Iron Company. The men wanted to organize in a union to improve pay and working conditions. The mine owners, including John D. Rockefeller, were opposed to workers' unions.

Sand Creek Massacre Footnote

As is often the case in battle, there were many conflicting stories of what really happened at Sand Creek. Was it a battle or was it a massacre? People are still debating the event today.

In Denver, there is a monument of a Civil War veteran that stands on the west steps of the state capitol building. It was erected in 1909. Beneath the statue is a list of twenty-two battles and engagements in which Colorado soldiers took part during the Civil War. Sand Creek is among those listed.

Many people feel that Sand Creek should not be on that list of Civil War battles. They think it was not a Civil War battle but a Native American massacre. So relatives of victims of Sand Creek came to Denver in November 2002 to add a plaque to the Civil War monument. The plaque reminds visitors that Sand Creek was not a Civil War

battle but was the site of the slaying of peaceful Native Americans. This "correction" to the historic record was made in the year 2002, exactly 138 years to the day of the surprise attack of Colonel John Chivington at Sand Creek.

Sand Creek Massacre.

The Ludlow Massacre

The Ludlow Massacre took place shortly after Woodrow Wilson took office as president of the United States. The conflict at Ludlow between workers and owners was a significant national event.

After going out on strike in September 1913, thousands of miners and their families had to vacate their company homes. But instead of leaving the area, many chose to stay on in a tent town and continued to ask for a workers' union. They not only wanted better pay, they also resented the fact that Colorado Fuel and Iron controlled everything in their lives. There were company-owned stores and company-controlled schools and libraries—even their church ministers were paid by Colorado Fuel and Iron.

Ludlow Memorial.

The Colorado Fuel and Iron Company was owned by the Rockefeller family. This rich family was influential in supporting the management of the company against the strikers.

Because the striking miners continued to stay in tent cities and protest, Colorado militiamen, coal company guards, and men hired as strikebreakers came to Ludlow. At first the miners greeted them with cheers. They

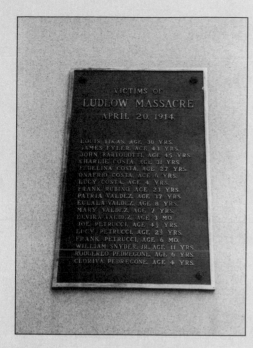

Ludlow Massacre plaque.

thought the militia had come to help them. Then they realized that the militia was there to fight them. The militia attacked on April 20, 1914, using an armored car mounted with a machine gun to shoot at the miners. The battle lasted for fourteen hours.

Some miners and family members were killed by gunshot wounds, but a larger number were suffocated. Women and children had taken shelter in a pit dug for their safety under their tent. When kerosene was poured on the tents and set ablaze, some of the people hiding in the pits suffocated. Between twenty and forty miners and their family members were killed.

National attention focused on the strike and the massacre. Writers such as Upton Sinclair and Carl Sandburg spoke out in favor of the miners. During the next few days, the striking miners continued to fight against the mine guards. Some troops disobeyed orders to go and join the fight against the miners. A few railroad workers refused to transport soldiers to Ludlow.

The striking miners attacked mines and company towns from Trinidad to Walsenburg. President Wilson finally sent federal troops to disarm both sides. Seven months later, the strike ended in defeat of the workers.

The United Mine Workers of America built a monument at the Ludlow site. It honors the struggle of workers in the United States. After the strike at Ludlow was broken, a company union was formed as a result of the miners' efforts. While not a strong, independent voice for the miners, the company union did achieve some improvements in working conditions.

Caribou

The ghost town of Caribou is located about five miles west of Nederland. Sam Conger discovered silver in Caribou in 1860. At the time, he did not know how valuable it was. He came back to the area nine years later with five other men. They discovered rich deposits of silver and laid claim to the Caribou Mine. By the next spring, 100 miners were camping on Caribou Hill. Until the Caribou Mine shut down in 1884, it was the richest silver mine in the Front Range.

Cabin near Caribou, Boulder County.

The town of Caribou began to grow. It became Caribou City in September 1870. It had a Methodist Church, several hotels, a grocery store, saloons, and a bakery. There was regular stage service to Central City. The town was in a cold and windy spot located in a high mountain meadow at 9,800 feet. In winter there were huge snowdrifts with snow so deep that people had to climb through second-story windows to get into their houses.

Silver mining in Caribou reached its peak in 1875. By that time there were almost 3,000 people in the town. After the mines shut down, people left. Two fires destroyed buildings until all that remains today is a cemetery and the stone ruins of an old hotel and assay office.

Como

Como is located about ten miles northeast of Fairplay, Colorado. George W. Lechner discovered a rich vein of coal there in 1871. He hauled loads of coal to Fairplay, and then finally sold his mine to the railroads. Several other coal properties were found within a few miles. In addition, there were some gold mines to the west.

In 1879, Como became a tent city for railroad construction crews. The men lived there while laying tracks for the Denver, South Park, and Pacific Railway. The town of about 500 or 600 people grew to 6,000 people during the building of the railroad.

Como was a division point for trains coming in from Denver. One branch carried trains to Breckenridge. The other went to Gunnison by way of the Alpine Tunnel. A huge roundhouse was built. The remains of that building can still be seen. Repair shops were located at Como, and the coal mines supplied the railroad with fuel.

Como had hotels and churches and a school. After 1909, people began to leave Como. A fire destroyed the railroad shops. The trains stopped making winter trips through the Alpine Tunnel, and then the roundhouse was closed. The railroad stopped traveling across the high alpine park. Now only a few people live in Como in summer homes.

Independence

Independence was a mining camp. Some people say that Dick Irwin or William Belden made the gold strike here. Others say that it was Charles Bennet who led the group that found gold. Over the years, the mine and the town had many names including Chipeta, Mount Hope, Sparkell, and Mammoth City. Finally it was called Independence. It was named for the Independence lode that had been found on the Fourth of July.

This gold strike was made five miles west of the summit of Hunter's Pass. This pass soon came to be known as Independence Pass. This road was hard to travel. Its highest point is 12,095 feet. No railroad ever reached Independence, but there was stagecoach service between there and Leadville.

The Big Storm at Independence

The town of Independence is at 10,830 feet. It's cold and snowy, and life is hard in winter. A rich lode of gold was discovered there on July 4, 1879, and in a short time, a town of 300 sprang up. By 1882, there were 1,500 residents and more than forty businesses. A miner could get room and board for $2 at a rooming house on Main Street.

From 1881 until 1882, $190,000 worth of gold was taken from Independence. But the next year, only $2,000 worth of gold was mined. As the gold played out, the residents left, until there were fewer than 100 people living there in 1888.

During the winter of 1899, a terrible snowstorm hit Independence. The town was cut off from everything, and the miners who were left in town were running out of food. Desperate, they tore up some cabins and made themselves seventy-five pairs of skis. The whole group skied to Aspen, more than thirty miles away.

A few mines near Independence continued working until 1900. Even after that, prospectors sometimes came hunting gold, but the town finally became deserted. Today, ruins of the camp can be seen in a meadow far below Independence Pass.

St. Elmo

St. Elmo is now a ghost town, but once it was home to mines that produced millions of dollars worth of ore. St. Elmo is in Chalk Creek Canyon about sixteen miles west of Nathrop. Once the town had between 1,000 and 2,000 people living in it. Today, much of the old main street is still there. The St. Elmo school is in a clump of trees about two blocks back from the main street.

In the late 1870s, St. Elmo was first called Forest City. Because there were other cities with that name, the post office wanted a new name for the town, and it was renamed St. Elmo. During its boom years in the 1880s and 1890s, there were five hotels, businesses, and a newspaper office.

Some say that gold was discovered there by Dr. Abner Wright and John Royal. But others tell a more colorful tale. They suggest that two prospectors with the name Murphy struck gold here. One of these brothers had a wife named Mary, and the other had a wife named Jennie. While one brother returned to the East to get his wife, the other sold the valuable Mary Murphy Mine for just a few thousand dollars. These historians maintain that when she got to Colorado, instead of being the wife of a wealthy mine owner, Mary Murphy had to get a job as a dishwasher.

Many people in St. Elmo worked at the Mary Murphy Mine just three miles away. But the town was also important for railroading. The Denver, South Park, and Pacific Railroads used St. Elmo as its railhead. In December 1880, the railroad reached St. Elmo from Buena Vista. It provided passenger and freight service until 1926. The line ran all the way through the Alpine Tunnel.

Activities for Further Exploration

1. To find out more about Bent's Fort and the sort of trading that went on there, a useful Internet site is http://www.nps.gov/beol/pphtml/forkids.html. If you write or call to make arrangements in advance, men and women serve as guides at Bent's Fort to take people on tours through the fort and talk about the blacksmith's shop, the kitchen, the trading post, and other special features.

2. Sand Creek was a famous event in Colorado's history. There is not complete agreement about what really happened there, but most people agree it was not a proud moment in state history. For information about the Battle of Sand Creek, you might visit the Internet at http://www.pbs.org/weta/thewest/resources/archives/four/sandcrk.htm. Many books have been written on this topic. One is *Black Kettle: The Cheyenne Chief Who Sought Peace but Found War* by Thom Hatch, 2004.

3. Ludlow is now a ghost town, but at one time it was a bustling coal mining town. Lots of pictures showing how Ludlow once looked can be found on the Internet at http://www.ghosttowngallery.com/htme/ludlowco.htm.

4. Como was once a thriving railroad town. To learn more about it, a good resource is *Railroads of Colorado: Your Guide to Colorado Historic Trains and Railway Sites* by Claude A. Wiatrowski.

Chapter 3
Prehistory Colorado

Dinosaur Tracks

The Rocky Mountains are the youngest of the world's great mountains. Scientists believe the Rocky Mountains are about 65 million years old. They cut right through the state of Colorado.

Before these mountains formed, an ocean covered the land. There are many places in Colorado where you can find fossils of animals that once lived in the sea. And there are places in Colorado where you can find traces of dinosaurs, too.

Animal Fossils

Fossils of prehistoric turtles, ancient horses, saber-toothed tigers, and a giant rhinoceros have been found in Colorado. These tell us about the early animals that lived here. *Apatosaurus* (formerly called *Brontosaurus*) and *Stegosaurus* lived in the Boulder Valley. Bones of *Apatosaurus* were found near De Beque. Remains of a *Tyrannosaurus rex* were found near La Junta.

Plant Fossils

There are also plant fossils. These include ferns and palm leaves. The coal beds, which were later mined in Lafayette, Louisville, and Marshall in Colorado, come from plants buried in the ground long ago. Most commonly, fossil leaves are found. Seeds, twigs, flowers, and even pollen grains are also present. These are life-sized. There are also petrified stumps of redwoods at some sites.

Prehistoric People

There are many opinions about how people arrived in North America. A recent idea is that people may have come by boat into North America from Asia. To do this, they would have had to find ice-free patches of water. A few skeletons and tools found along the West Coast of North America support this idea.

Picketwire Canyonland Dinosaur Tracksite

We learn about prehistory by carefully studying remains from the past. These remains can be bits of pottery, tools, bones, and even footprints. The largest dinosaur tracksite in North America is located in Colorado in the Comanche National Grasslands south of La Junta. The track-bearing rock parallels the Purgatoire River for one-quarter of a mile.

How were these dinosaur footprints left in the rock? About 150 million years ago, there was a huge freshwater lake in southeastern Colorado. The climate was warm and wet. Hundreds of dinosaurs lived in this area. These included meat-eating dinosaurs, duckbills, and long-necked plant eaters. They left their footprints in the soupy mud at the edge of the lake in what is now a rock layer called the Morrison Rock Formation.

Eventually, the muddy flats were buried and turned to stone with the indentations of the dinosaur prints left in them. Over time, wind and rain exposed the footprints again. Today a visitor can see more than 1,300 dinosaur footprints at the Picketwire Canyonlands Dinosaur Tracksite. Scientists have also found there the remains of freshwater clams and fish, and the limestone layers in the area record ripple marks from the ancient lake.

Dinosaur National Monument

Dinosaur National Monument is shared between the states of Utah and Colorado. It is located near Vernal, Utah, and Dinosaur, Colorado. About two-thirds of the monument is in Colorado. The area is about 210,000 acres in size. The monument protects the largest single deposit of dinosaur bones from the Jurassic Period ever found.

The first of these fossils was discovered in 1909 by Earl Douglass, a paleontologist who worked for the Carnegie Museum of Pittsburgh, Pennsylvania. Douglass spent years working in this area, digging up dinosaur bones and shipping them to Pittsburgh. His work was well publicized, and President Woodrow Wilson proclaimed the site as Dinosaur National Monument in 1915.

Scientists think that 150 million years ago, a large river flowed through this area. Many dinosaurs lived and died here. Their bones and bodies were carried off by the river and buried in sand and gravel. During the ages that followed, the river dried up. Layers of sand and mud solidified into rock. The buried dinosaur bones filled with dissolved minerals and fossilized.

Over time, the layers of rock in this area tilted upward. Due to exposure to wind and rain, rock layers containing the long-buried dinosaur bones were uncovered and appeared near the surface where Douglass and other scientists found them.

The steep cliff face, or quarry, is now enclosed in a large building that protects the fossils. Bones of eleven kinds of dinosaurs were found there. Scientists study the bones and teeth and take an educated guess as to what these animals looked like and how they lived.

About 65 million years ago, the dinosaurs died out. People still wonder what happened to cause this. There are many theories and many questions. Did the weather become too hot or cold? Did plant eaters starve? Did other creatures eat the dinosaur eggs? Did an asteroid crash into Earth and darken the skies with dust? Although we may never be sure what made them extinct, we can still study the remains of these creatures at Dinosaur National Monument.

Others think that people came to North America by a land bridge that connected Alaska and Siberia. Thousands of years ago, much of Canada was buried under ice. The last ice age lasted from 1.8 million until only 11,000 years ago. During that time it was too cold for the snow and ice to melt. Sea levels fell because there was no melting water to fill them. Oceans shrank away from the coastlines.

As the waters fell, a wide strip of land appeared between Siberia and Alaska. The strip of land was about 1,000 feet wide. It was right where the Bering Sea is today. Scientists sometimes call this strip of land Beringia. They believe that somewhere between 28,000 and 10,000 years ago, animals walked across this strip of land.

In this way, large animals such as mammoths, bison, and caribou reached North America. The Asian people who hunted these herds of animals followed them. Scientists call these early people Paleo-Indians. Some of these people came down through Canada into what is now the United States.

When the great sheets of ice were melting, people were living in Colorado. What little we know about these people, we learn from what they left behind. Scientists have found spear points, animal bones, and simple tools. These give us an idea of how these ancient people might have lived.

The Dent Site
Scientists came to dig at the Dent Site in Weld County, Colorado, in 1932 and 1933. They came because a railroad foreman and a priest who were out walking along a gully found some very large animal bones and spear points sticking out of the dirt.

The scientists who came to investigate the area found the remains of fourteen mammoths. Mammoths were animals that looked something like today's elephants. They stood about twelve feet tall and weighed around 10,000 pounds. In addition to the animal bones, scientists found three spear points that had been shaped by humans. Scientists believe ancient people used these spear points to kill mammoths for food.

Clovis People

Blackwater Draw is between the towns of Clovis and Portales in New Mexico. Scientists found a cave there that they called Ventana Cave. This cave may have been a camp for Paleo-Indians. Scientists found grinding stones in the cave that may have been used to grind bean pods and seeds.

In the area, scientists found the bones of prehistoric bison, mammoths, and ground sloths. They also found spearheads that might have been used in hunting the animals. The points were the same kind that were found at the Dent Site in Colorado.

Clovis sites have been dated at about 9000 B.C. by radiocarbon. Clovis groups are thought to be the earliest dated human populations in the Americas. Scientists called these early humans Clovis people, and they called the spearheads Clovis points.

Clovis points are long, thin blades with a channel on each side. The points were attached to a spear, which was thrown by an atlatl.

Folsom People

Near Fort Collins, Colorado, there is an area called the Lindenmeier Site. It is now a national historic landmark. Spearheads found at the site are called Folsom points. Folsom points get their name because they look much like some that were found at Folsom, New Mexico. Folsom points have a wide groove from the point to the base along both sides of the spearhead.

The discovery of these points was made by George McJunkin. He was an African American cowboy. He made his discovery in 1908 after a flash flood. The flood uncovered unusually large bison bones. In the same area in 1926, more spear points and bison bones were found.

Finding the Folsom points and animal bones together made scientists think that this early man was a hunter, too. They gave the name "Folsom people" to the early people who hunted with this kind of spearhead. From the different bones that were found, scientists think that Folsom people hunted bison, antelope, and rabbits. Folsom people may have followed herds of animals over a large area.

43

The Atlatl

An atlatl is a spear-throwing stick. The word "atlatl" probably came from the Aztecs. An atlatl is a wooden stick that has a handle on one end and a hook on the other. The hook attaches to the back end of a spear. The hunter would throw with an overhand motion like a baseball pitcher. This increased the force of the thrown spear.

When the Paleo-Indians came into North America, perhaps from the land bridge that joined Asia and North America, there were herds of animals on this tundralike land. Some of these animals were very large. They included the mammoth, the mastodon, and huge long-horned bison. Rather than live in one place, these Paleo-Indians moved about, following the herds of animals.

The people who hunted these animals probably first used spears to kill them. But they later learned to use the atlatl, or spear-thrower, which allowed them to hunt from a safer distance and to be more effective. The thrower acted as an extension of the arm. It added speed and accuracy to the flying dart or spear. Most of these darts or spears had replaceable parts, so that the point of the dart would stay in the animal.

At a site 150 miles east of Denver, Colorado, scientists have found a place where several hundred bison were killed. The site is estimated to be 10,000 years old. Among the bones were projectile points that appear to have been re-sharpened and used to butcher and skin the bison.

There are people today who still use the atlatl. The Australian aborigines use several styles of atlatls. One that is used in eastern Australia is called the *woomera*.

People in the United States have become interested in the atlatl, too. They have learned to make and use them in contests. A World Atlatl Association was chartered in Colorado in 1988. In a typical year more than 100 atlatl contests are held in Europe and the United States.

In addition to spear points and bones, scrapers and beads were found at the Lindenmeier Site. These are the oldest known beads in North America. It is estimated that they date from about 9500 B.C. Half of these beads were put in the Denver Museum of Nature & Science. The other half of the beads were placed in the Smithsonian Museum in Washington.

Yuma People

Other spearheads have been found in Colorado near Yuma in the northeast corner of the state. There are no grooves on these spear-heads, and the points are narrower than Folsom points. This type of spearhead is also known as a Yuma point or Eden point. This type of spear point has also been found in Wyoming, Nebraska, and Montana.

Scientists call the early people who used these spearheads Yuma people. Yuma points were made by chipping flakes off stone. The edges were sharp, and the points were usually made of flint. Sometimes they were made of other materials including quartz. Probably Folsom points and Yuma points were both used as spears.

Early Basketmakers

The Paleo-Indians who came to the Four Corners area in Colorado about 11,000 years ago were hunters. Although they had no knowledge of the bow and arrow, they used the atlatl. Then about 8,500 years ago, the lives of the Paleo-Indians changed from primarily big game hunting to a hunting and gathering lifestyle. Although they continued to hunt small animals, the people began gathering plant foods and preparing meal, or flour, from wild grass seeds to add to their diet of meat. Grinding stones have been found from this period of history.

Then between about 4,000 and 1,800 years ago, the people changed again. Although they still moved about and went on hunting trips, they began cultivating corn. They probably traded from Mexico for these corn seeds. And as they planted and harvested corn, they built small villages and moved about less.

Between 100 B.C. and A.D. 1300 a group of people moved into southwestern Colorado. The Hopi, Zuni, Acoma, and Navajo groups of Native Americans who live in the Southwest today trace their history back to these people. They are called Ancestral Puebloans and they are known as the "Basketmakers." Their coiled baskets were made so well that they would hold water. The Basketmakers lived in caves and pit houses. They hunted with bows and arrows.

By A.D. 800, the people living in southwestern Colorado were also farmers. They raised turkeys and grew corn and squash. They knew how to irrigate their crops. These people could weave cloth and used yucca fibers and other plants in their weaving.

The Ancestral Puebloans were great builders. They built their homes in cliffs. They used stone masonry and built many-storied buildings of adobe, a mixture of clay and straw. Their homes look something like apartments.

Many ruins believed to have belonged to the Ancient Puebloans have been found in Colorado. The Chimney Rock Site is east of Bayfield in the San Juan National Forest. There scientists found the ruins of a dozen villages. Several hundred people probably lived in this area around the tenth century.

Crow Canyon is another site of the Ancient Puebloans. The ruins here are northwest of the city of Cortez. Pueblo ruins and rock art have been found here.

A third site is the Lowry Ruins, named for the homesteader George Lowry. The site contains ruins of forty rooms and eight ceremonial kivas. Parts of the ruins are three stories high. The area was home to about 100 people. It was probably occupied between A.D. 1050 and A.D. 1300. Digging in the ruins took place in the 1930s by scientists who came from a museum in Chicago. The Lowry Ruins became a national historic landmark in 1967.

The most famous ruins of the Ancient Puebloan homes are found at Mesa Verde, Colorado. Mesa Verde is a Spanish name. *Mesa* means table; *verde* means green.

It was not until 1888 that Cliff Palace was discovered by

Charlie Mason and Richard Wetherill, two cattlemen. Now this area has been made into part of Mesa Verde National Park. There are 350 cliff dwellings in the park and more than 500 pueblos, or villages. Cliff Palace is like an apartment house with 200 rooms and twenty-three kivas. Many of the walls of the cliff dwellers were painted or scratched with designs and picture stories that can still be seen.

Cliff Palace, Mesa Verde National Park.

Scientists have determined that there was a very dry period from A.D. 1276 to A.D. 1299. This may have been one of the reasons that the Ancient Puebloan culture began to decline about this time. The people may have moved away because these many dry years killed their crops. Other scientists think they may have been attacked by another tribe. No one is certain. Although the reasons remain unclear, by 1300, people had left the area.

Those who are interested in learning more about the Ancestral Puebloans may visit the Anasazi Heritage Center in Dolores, Colorado. It is a museum run by the Bureau of Land Management and has interesting exhibits relating to these ancient people on display to the public.

Activities for Further Exploration

1. You might want to try your hand at making some pinch pots or coiled pots that resemble those used by prehistoric people. Once these small pots dry or are fired in a kiln, they could be filled with attractive dried flowers, grasses, or weeds to make a pretty home decoration. For pictures and directions for these pots, see on the Internet http://artswork.asu.edu/arts/students/navajo/lesson4.htm.

2. Make a model of some of the Mesa Verde Native American cliff dwellings or kivas. These models might be built with clay or made from cardboard. A useful resource showing what your cliff house should look like is *The Ancient Cliff Dwellers of Mesa Verde: A Close Look at the Anasazi* by Caroline Arnold with photography by Richard Hewett.

3. Learn more about Ancient Puebloan pottery and baskets and prehistoric arrowheads and simple tools. For an example of how baskets and pottery were made by the Ancient Puebloans, visit the Internet at http://www.sover.net/~barback/pots/pots.html.

4. Many prehistoric animals lived in Colorado. Stegosaurus is Colorado's state fossil. In 1877, a teacher found an enormous stegosaurus vertebra in Morrison, Colorado. A nearly complete stegosaurus skeleton was found by a teacher and students from Canon City High. To print out a picture of stegosaurus, go to http://www.zoomdinosaurs.com/subjects/dinosaurs/dino templates/Stegosaurus.shtml.

Chapter 4
Native Americans in Colorado:
The Ute, Arapaho, and Cheyenne

Many Native Americans were living in Colorado by the time the Europeans arrived. The two major groups were the Mountain Indians (the Ute) and the Plains Indians (the Arapaho and the Cheyenne).

The Mountain Indians

The Ute once lived throughout most of Colorado and Utah as well as in parts of Arizona and New Mexico. The word "Ute" comes from the Indian word *yuta*, which means "people of the mountains." In about A.D. 1500, the Ute moved into what is now Colorado. They settled in a large area that extended from the Utah border to the Great Plains.

Some of the Ute lived in the mesa country of western Colorado; others were in the pine-covered hills to the south. And the Ute also lived for at least part of the year in the Rocky Mountains.

The Ute needed large land areas because they moved about a good deal. They did very little farming, but were hunters and gatherers. They hunted small animals and birds and gathered seeds and berries and piñon nuts. They would camp for a time in a spot, then, when berries and animals grew scarce, the Ute would move their camp to a new place.

In the summer, the Ute went up into the mountains. There they continued to hunt and gather food. When the snows came, the Ute moved again. Some spent the winter on the eastern plains, while others moved to mesa and desert country. Winter was often a hard and hungry time for these people.

In winter, the Ute built dome-shaped shelters of willow branches that were tied and woven together and then covered in grass. These were called wickiups. The Ute kept warm by wearing deerskin clothing and using blankets made of rabbit fur. Even in the snow, they might be able to catch rabbits and other small animals to eat. But often during the wintertime, they lived by eating dried meat and berries that they had saved from summer.

As winter ended, Ute bands of families got together to celebrate spring. This was called the Bear Dance Celebration.

In summer, food was much more plentiful. The Ute dug up and ate wild onions and wild potatoes. They ate the fruit of the yucca plant. The yucca fruit is often called the "Ute banana." They also gathered wild berries and chokecherries. Occasionally they would plant corn and beans, which they harvested in the fall.

The Ute fished in streams and hunted birds, squirrels, rabbits, elk, and deer. In summer they slept out in the open, though sometimes they made shelters from the branches of trees.

The Ute lived together and traveled in family groups. These small groups included the parents, children, and

Utes on horseback.
Courtesy of the Tom Noel Collection

grandparents. Sometimes there were aunts, uncles, and cousins, too. Babies were carried on cradle boards.

When the children got older and could walk, they were no longer kept in cradle boards. The grandparents would often watch the younger children. This allowed the father to hunt, and it freed the mother to gather food and do the cooking and sewing.

The Ute dressed in plain buckskin clothing at first. Later they decorated their clothing with beads and porcupine quills and sometimes wore jewelry. They made necklaces from animal claws and made beads of stones, bones, and seeds.

Although the Ute spent most of their time in family units, they were part of a community, too. The larger community group was called a band. Each band had its own chief. The chief was advised by a council made up of the older men of the band.

There were seven major Ute bands. The Mouache lived in southern Colorado and New Mexico. The Capote lived in the San Luis Valley and in parts of New Mexico. The Weeminuche lived along the San Juan River in Colorado and in northwestern New Mexico. The Tabeguache Band lived in the valleys of the Gunnison and Uncompahgre Rivers in Colorado. The Grand River Ute lived along the Grand River in Colorado and Utah. The Yampa Band was in the Yampa River Valley. And the Uintah Ute lived in the western portion of the Uintah Basin.

The Spanish had brought horses to North America in the 1500s. When the Spanish rode these animals north from Mexico into New Mexico, the Ute saw horses for the first time. They saw how useful these animals were. Horses could carry loads from place to place, and they could be used in hunting.

The Ute soon got horses of their own. They might trade food and animal skins to get horses.

Chipeta and Ouray.
Courtesy of Denver Public Library, Western History Collection, Walker Art Studio, X-30600

Some Ute were captured by the Spanish and were forced to work on ranches. Other Ute worked willingly on Spanish ranches. Either way, they learned on ranches how to care for horses. When they

The Bear Dance Celebration

The bear signified strength and power to the Ute. The spring Bear Dance Celebration is a significant and sacred event to the tribal members. It is still celebrated today. The participants chant old songs and dance to rhythms in patterns that have been handed down from the past.

There are differing stories about the origins of the Bear Dance. In one legend, a Ute warrior is led by his dreams into the mountains where he sees a bear. The bear teaches him the sacred dance. In another story, a bear wakes from hibernation and sees a Ute hunter. The hunter spares the bear's life, and the bear teaches him the dance. And in yet another legend, two brothers are out hunting and come upon a dancing bear. One brother remains to watch and learn the dance.

In olden times and today, the Bear Dance symbolizes the connectedness of all life on earth. People gather to visit, tell stories, play games, and dance. While the dancing goes on, some men play growl sticks. Growl sticks are notched wood, stroked by bones. These wooden instruments make a rasping sound that sounds a little like a bear when it claws a tree.

The original Bear Dance Celebration lasted for several days. The celebration ends with a great feast, and then Ute families go their separate ways.

Cradle Boards

The use of cradle boards is common among Native Americans, especially those who were involved in hunting and gathering. The cradle board may have originated with the early Asian hunters who brought cradle boards with them when they migrated across the land bridge and into North America.

Different groups fashioned and decorated their cradle boards in distinctive ways, but their uses were similar.

The cradle boards protected the child, provided an easy means of transport, and freed the mother's arms to do daily chores. They allowed the child to see the world from mother's back or from where the board was propped up. A child usually was kept in a cradle board until he or she was about a year old.

Cradles were either cut from flat pieces of wood or woven with flexible willow or hazel twigs into a frame. The wood or frames were covered in buckskin. Sometimes there was a hood to protect the baby from the sun and weather. These cradles were about twenty by fourteen inches. Ute cradle boards are wide at the top and narrow at the bottom.

The cradle board was often carried on the mother's back by shoulder straps. Sometimes the board was hung from a tree, and when the family was traveling, the cradle board might be hung from the horse's saddle.

Some cradle boards were decorated in red, green, white, blue, and orange beadwork. Other cradles were decorated in porcupine quillwork. Soft materials such as lichen, moss, cattail down, and shredded bark were used for cushioning.

In many ways these old cradle boards remind us of modern day plastic infant seats or cloth slings. And just as modern babies often enjoy looking up from their cribs at dangling mobiles, so did Native American infants look up at feathers or toys hanging from the hood piece of their cradle boards. Young Native American girls played with dolls tucked in miniature cradle boards, much as a modern child might play with a doll in a buggy or small crib.

left, they often took horses back to their families. Sometimes the Ute stole horses from the Spanish, and sometimes they stole horses from Comanche tribes. As the Ute began using horses, their way of life changed.

Once the Ute had horses, they learned to hunt herds of buffalo. Getting food was much easier. This meant that instead of living in small family units, the Ute began living in larger bands. They made tepees from buffalo skins and used these for homes instead of wickiups. When they moved camp, the horses could move the hides and tepee poles.

Large bands of Ute were a good fighting force. Led by their chiefs, they sometimes attacked other Native American tribes and stole horses and goods. The chiefs often wore bonnets made from eagle feathers.

Chief Ouray was a leader of the Ute. Today you can see a picture of Chief Ouray in a stained glass window in the state capitol in Denver. A city, county, and mountain have all been named Ouray. The chief's wife was named Chipeta. Near Montrose, Colorado, is an Indian museum. A beaded buckskin shirt that once belonged to Chief Ouray is in that museum.

The Plains Indians

The Ute often warred with the Plains Indians, the Arapaho and Cheyenne. At one time, the Arapaho lived to the east of Colorado. They lived in villages and planted corn. Then they moved into Colorado. They were among the first Native Americans to arrive in Colorado.

When the Cheyenne first moved onto the plains of Colorado, they lived in houses made of sticks that were covered in mud and they hunted buffalo. By the early 1800s there were many Cheyenne and Arapaho in Colorado, and they became friends with one another. They spoke with each other in sign language. In time, some learned to speak both languages, and they would often visit together.

When they moved, the early Cheyenne and Arapaho had no horses to assist in carrying their things. Rather they used dogs to help them. They built something called a travois. It was made of two poles that were tied to the dog's back. Clothes and light loads were tied to the poles, and the dogs pulled these.

The Cheyenne and the Arapaho lived mostly by hunting buffalo. Both the Arapaho and Cheyenne followed the buffalo herds from spring until fall. Because they were hunting on foot, they would have to sneak up on buffalo at a watering hole. Or they would try to surround a herd and frighten some of them into running off a cliff.

Then, like the Ute, the Cheyenne and Arapaho got horses that were first brought into North America by the Spanish. They began using horses as pack animals. Horses would pull the tepee poles and buffalo skins from camp to camp.

They also rode their horses when they went to hunt. When a buffalo herd was found, a large group of men went out after them, chasing the buffalo, using bows and arrows, and throwing lances at them. They killed as many buffalo as they needed.

After the buffalo were killed, the women and children came to help. They would skin the animals and cut up the meat. Then the hides and meat were taken back to camp where the women would tan buffalo hides.

First, they scraped the hides to remove the fat and meat. Sometimes they left the hair on the pieces that would be used for tepee coverings. But for pieces used to make clothes, they removed the hair. Hides were rubbed with animal brains and soapweed and then dried in the sun. Finally, the hides were softened by being pulled over a rope of buffalo sinew.

Pieces of buffalo meat were roasted over the fire. Smaller pieces were used to make a stew. Some of the meat was dried in strips. Pemmican was made by pounding buffalo meat into a powder and mixing it with dried berries to give it flavor. Then it was mixed with fat and cooked in little cakes. The Plains Indians also ate berries, seeds, and roots.

The buffalo supplied the Arapaho and Cheyenne with other things as well. Cups and spoons were made from buffalo horns.

Digging and scraping tools were made from bones, and buffalo fat was used to make soap.

It took ten to twenty buffalo hides to make a tepee. The large tepees could hold a family and all its things. The beds were covered in buffalo robes. Extra clothes and robes were stored under the beds. In the middle of the tepee was the cooking fire. A hole in the top of the tepee let the smoke out. Sometimes pictures were painted on the tepees. These pictures told about brave deeds.

Dried meat hung from the lodge poles. Early trappers called dried meat "jerky." Jerky keeps for months. Some campers and hikers today buy or make beef jerky to take with them on mountain trips.

In the summer, the tribe would come together. Young children would be carried on their mothers' backs on cradle boards. Sometimes the whole tribe would go out on a buffalo hunt. Afterwards, they would visit, feast, and dance the Sun Dance.

The Arapaho and Cheyenne always lived in villages. By living in groups, they could protect each other from enemies. Each tribe had several villages or bands. Other Native Americans lived on the plains of eastern Colorado. They were the Apache, Comanche, Crow, Kiowa, Pawnee, and Sioux.

The principal chief of the Southern Arapaho, and a friend to Chief Niwot, was a chief named Little Raven. He helped the Arapaho and Cheyenne make a lasting peace with the plains tribes south of the Arkansas.

The word "Arapaho" means "people with many tattoos." The Arapaho men often had tattoos of three small circles across their chest. Women sometimes had a tattoo on their foreheads. To make a tattoo, they cut their skin with the sharp point of a cactus. The point would be rubbed in water and ashes. The color of the ashes stayed in the scar and made the tattoo.

Roman Nose was another famous Cheyenne war chief. He is credited with many attacks on emigrants going West on the Oregon Trail.

Chief Niwot

Chief Niwot was an Arapaho Indian. In the Arapaho language, *niwot* means "left hand." He and his tribe lived in Left Hand Valley near Haystack Mountain just north of what is now the city of Boulder.

In the mid-1800s, several forts were built along the Arkansas and the South Platte Rivers. These included Bent's Fort, Fort St. Vrain, Fort Laramie, Fort Lupton, Fort Vasquez, and Fort Jackson.

Chief Niwot.

John Poisol, from Kentucky, was one of the men who worked at Bent's Fort. Left Hand's sister, MaHom, married this white trader, and Poisol took an interest in his wife's younger brother and began tutoring him in English. Left Hand had a gift for languages and, in addition to English, learned to speak several Indian languages.

When Captain Thomas Aikens and his party of twenty gold seekers from Nebraska came into the Boulder Valley in 1859, Chief Niwot and his people were camped not far to the north. The chief came and talked to the new arrivals in English.

Chief Niwot often went up Left Hand Canyon in the summer to Gold Lake, which is currently a summer resort near the little town of Nederland. A large rock south of the lake is called Niwot's Rock. Chief Niwot was killed at the Sand Creek Massacre in 1864. A statue of Chief Niwot is in a Boulder park not far from the town's main library.

According to legend, Chief Niwot placed a curse on Boulder. He said, "People seeing the beauty of the Boulder Valley will want to stay, and their staying will be the undoing of the beauty."

Reservations

At first the Ute got along well with the Spanish and Mexican governments. They traded and were peaceful. The Old Spanish Trail was used as a regular trading route in the 1820s. But in the 1830s, when Mexicans settled on Indian lands, the Ute and Navajo raided the Mexican settlements.

As more and more people moved onto land that once was home to only Native Americans, problems increased. These problems were not unexpected. Early in American history, people such as Thomas Jefferson worried about the future of Native Americans. He and many other leaders of the time thought that if Indians would adopt Christianity and learn the principles of property ownership, farming, and cattle raising, they would succeed in the growing new country. But many Native Americans did not want to abandon their beliefs and culture and adopt the white man's ways.

Some reservations were established by the United States government as early as 1786. While the reservations provided Native Americans with homes and land to cultivate, they also established control over them and confined them to given limits. Reservation life meant a radical change in the habits and culture of Native Americans. It often meant that the Native Americans were moved far away from their original homes into unfamiliar land. Reservations also excluded Native Americans from actively taking part in the political and social mainstream.

In 1825, President Monroe drew up a plan for the removal of all tribes east of the Mississippi to the same general region, called "Indian Territory," which included present-day Oklahoma and Kansas.

The U.S. government and the Ute signed an agreement in 1849 after the Mexican-American War. The Ute agreed not to leave their usual territory without permission. But in 1859, when the Colorado gold rush began, thousands of settlers rushed in. They took up hunting land that had belonged to the Ute. Buffalo were scarce and the Ute lacked enough food.

The government set up agencies to give the Native Americans food and supplies. The agencies also encouraged farming.

Reservations were established in Colorado by a variety of executive orders between 1863 and 1895. As a result, a reservation was set up for the Ute in 1863, but many changes were made over the years. For example, in March 1878, Nathan Meeker was appointed Indian agent of the White River Ute Reservation. He tried to turn the Ute into farmers. When they resisted, he called in the army in September 1879 to deal with troublemakers. In response, a group of warriors killed Meeker and seven others from the agency. The Ute were then evicted and moved to a reservation in Utah.

Today many Native Americans choose to live on reservations in Colorado and in other nearby states. If they do, they live with groups of their own people. And they have certain special rights on the reservation lands. During the civil rights movement of the 1960s, Native Americans on reservations began making demands. Some tribal members got compensation to help make up for earlier government wrongdoing. Native American artifacts and human remains that had been kept in some museums were ordered returned to tribes for appropriate tribal ceremonies. The Native Americans were given legal and political control within their borders. Many gained the right to manage hunting, fishing, and natural resources within their reservations. These steps represent major improvements for those who live on reservations today.

The Uintah and Ouray Reservation is located in northeast Utah about 150 miles east of Salt Lake City. It is home to the Uintah, Uncompahgre, and White River Bands of Ute. The reservation contains 4.5 million acres. Its headquarters is at Fort Duchesne, Utah.

The Southern Ute Reservation, with tribal headquarters in Ignacio, is located in southwestern Colorado. It stretches along the Colorado border with New Mexico. In the year 2000, it was home to more than 10,000 Ute. Most are from the Mouache Band and the Capote Band. The U.S. Bureau of Reclamation is now building the Animas-LaPlata water project outside Durango to satisfy the early water rights of the Southern Ute and Mountain Ute.

The Ute Mountain Ute Reservation is in southwestern

Colorado and northern New Mexico. It is made up mostly of the Ute from the Weeminuche Band. In the year 2000, more than 1,600 Ute lived there on 553,000 acres. The tribal headquarters is located in Towaoc, Colorado.

The Cheyenne went to the Northern Cheyenne Reservation in southeast Montana. It covers 445,000 acres. More than 4,000 Northern Cheyenne live on or near the reservation. The tribal headquarters is in Lame Deer.

Many of the Southern Arapaho and Northern and Southern Cheyenne were sent to a reservation in Oklahoma. An agreement with the United States government in October 1890 set aside 529,682 acres there for 3,294 Native Americans.

The Wind River Reservation in Montana is home to the Northern Arapaho. It covers 2,268,008 acres with 5,953 tribal members. The tribal headquarters is in Fort Washakie, Wyoming.

Activities for Further Exploration

1. Southwestern Native American pottery is very beautiful. Learn more about Native American arts. A useful resource is *Southwestern Pottery: Anasazi to Zuni* by Allan Hayes and John Blom. Another is *Navajo Weaving Way: The Path from Fleece to Rug* by Noel Bennett and Tiana Bighorse. For a good Internet site showing southwestern arts, visit http://www.native-languages.org/southwestern.htm.

2. Some Native Americans lived in tepees. For directions on making models of tepees using twigs and brown paper grocery bags, go to http://www.enchantedlearning.com/crafts/na/teepee.

3. The designs painted on tepees of the Plains Indians often depicted buffalo hunts and battles. Make a model of a tepee as explained above or draw a tepee and paint symbols on it. To learn more about tepee designs, go to http://www.mce.k12tn.net/Indians/reports4/plains.htm.

4. There are many Native American myths and tales. Read and enjoy some of these. Possible titles include *Crow Chief, A Plains Indian Story* by Paul Goble; *Coyote and the Laughing Butterflies* by Harriet Peck Taylor; *The Girl Who Married the Moon: Tales from Native North America* told by Joseph Bruchac and Gayle Ross; and *Myths, Legends & Tales* by Phyllis J. Perry.

Chapter 5
Spanish Exploration in and around Colorado

It is hard to know exactly when the Spanish first explored Colorado because written records from so long ago are scarce and sometimes inaccurate. We do know that the Spanish were in the American Southwest very early.

An explorer named Cabeza de Vaca was part of an expedition in 1527 and was shipwrecked off the coast of Florida. He and three companions, including a black Moor named Estevanico, survived and landed on Galveston Island near what is now the Texas coast. They came ashore and explored the new country, including Texas and northern Mexico, for six to eight years.

When they finally got to Mexico City, they talked about things that had happened during their journeys. No one knows for sure if they were exaggerating or telling the truth. They told of being held captive by Native Americans and they reported hearing about large cities of many-storied houses to the north that had doorways studded with emeralds and turquoise. Cabeza de Vaca published an account of his journeys in 1555.

The Search for the Seven Golden Cities

Tales of seven golden cities north of Mexico have existed for a long time. The oldest version of the fabled cities is based on the belief that hundreds of years ago, seven bishops fled Spain for the New World after the Moorish conquest and brought with them gold, gems, and religious articles.

In 1529, Brother Marcos de Niza, a Franciscan priest, went to look for the rumored golden cities. He took with him as a guide the black slave called Estevanico, who had been with Cabeza de Vaca. Estevanico had survived by using his wits. When with Native Americans, he often said he was a healer and apparently had some success in curing the sick.

On the 1529 expedition, Estevanico usually rode ahead of the Spanish explorers. He dressed elaborately and enjoyed being treated almost like a god whenever he arrived in a village. But his fancy dress and sense of importance finally got him into trouble when he reached a Zuni village. He was shaking a beaded gourd decorated in owl feathers that he used in his healing ceremony. Owls were considered evil omens by these people. Instead of being well treated, Estevanico was thought to be a threat and perhaps even a witch and was killed by the Native Americans.

After his guide was killed, Brother Marcos decided not to go into the unfriendly Zuni village, but he observed it from a distance. Some suggest that Brother Marcos saw the village during a sunset and mistook the sun shining on bits of silica on the adobe walls as having the glimmer of gold. Whether he really thought he saw a golden city or whether he made the story up, upon his return he claimed to have seen a village with buildings made of gold, although no one ever returned and found it.

Similar stories of treasure persist right up to the present time. Some believe that there is gold beneath Victorio Peak north of Las Cruces, New Mexico. These gold seekers argue that there are petroglyphs on rocks and caves in the area that are treasure maps left by Brother Marcos de Niza. They believe that if they interpret and follow the treasure maps, they will find gold that was mined in these caves and traded with the Aztecs.

When Antonio de Mendoza became the king's viceroy, or representative, from Spain in Mexico in 1535, his friend Coronado came with him. It wasn't long before they heard stories about rich cities filled with gold and silver in the lands just to the north of Mexico.

These seven rich cities were legendary only, but rumors of them did encourage Spanish exploration. Viceroy Mendoza kept sending men to find these cities. He wanted the golden jewelry and other objects he'd heard about in the stories. Hernando de Alarcon led one group of explorers that went along the coast by boat. They sailed up the Gulf of California and discovered the mouth of the Colorado River on August 26, 1540.

Coronado and his men set out to explore on land. He and his scouting parties went along the upper Rio Grande. They rode into

New Mexico, Arizona, Texas, and perhaps even Kansas. But historians think they probably did not explore what is now the state of Colorado.

Because neither of the explorers, by sea or land, returned with riches, the Spanish lost interest for a time in the lands to the north. Unfriendly Indians also discouraged them, with raids by the Apache, Comanche, Ute, and Navajo. In the years following, it is likely that some Spanish people came into the San Luis Valley in Colorado, but there are no written records of this.

Then the stories about the golden cities were heard again. The king of Spain was interested in this new land and wanted gold. He made Juan de Oñate governor of an area called New Mexico. In 1598, Oñate led 400 colonists into New Mexico. His group included soldiers, priests, farmers, women, and children, as well as domestic animals. They brought eighty cartloads of belongings. He established the headquarters of the New Mexico colony at San Juan Pueblo in the northern Rio Grande valley.

And so in 1598, nine years before the English made a settlement in Jamestown, there were Spanish colonies along the Rio Grande River. These colonists were just fifty miles south of what is now the Colorado state line.

After the first settlement, many other little villages grew up, but Oñate knew that the king had not sent him there to live quietly in a village. He began exploring, still looking for the cities of gold. He traveled hundreds of miles, visiting what is now Texas and New Mexico. And Oñate explored the area that is now Trinidad, Colorado, and reached the San Luis Valley. He may have gone as far north as where Denver is now located, but he did not find the fabled cities of gold.

The Native Americans in this area were often treated badly by the early Spanish. Some were made to work in the fields. Others worked as slaves in mines. The Native Americans became so unhappy that they revolted in 1680.

During the revolt, the Native Americans seized guns, killed the Spanish in the Taos, New Mexico, area, and burned missions. They filled in the mines and tried to destroy everything the Spanish had built. The Native Americans drove the Spanish back to Santa Fe, and from there, they drove them south of the Rio Grande and all the way back into Mexico.

For a time, the Native Americans in the New Mexico area were free of the Spanish. Then the king of Spain sent Diego de Vargas to retake his lands in New Mexico. Vargas arrived in El Paso in February 1691. He spent months training an army before he went north and retook Santa Fe in September 1692. In another two years, he had retaken Taos and other towns in the area.

Toward the end of 1694, Vargas rebuilt a mission in the San Luis Valley. That same year while searching for gold in the Sangre de Cristo Mountains, he explored the area around the Great Sand Dunes in Colorado.

The San Luis Valley: A Place of Superlatives and Supernatural
The town of San Luis, the first permanent town in Colorado, was founded in the spring of 1851 and was named after a Catholic saint.

The San Luis Valley is the world's largest alpine valley with an average altitude of 7,500 feet. Originally home to the Ute, this valley is bordered by mountains. The Sangre de Cristos make up the eastern border. The Rocky Mountains are to the north and northeast, and in the west are the San Juans. The Rio Grande River begins as a small stream in the San Juan Mountains on the western side of the valley, which is approximately 125 miles long and sixty-five miles wide.

After white settlers came, Fort Massachusetts was founded to provide the people with protection against hostile Indians. Fort Massachusetts was replaced in 1858 by Fort Garland, which is about sixteen miles north of San Luis. This fort held more than 100 men. Kit Carson was the post commandant for a year in 1866, and he succeeded for a time in keeping things peaceful with the Native Americans. The fort was finally abandoned in 1883.

Today the San Luis Valley is known for its agriculture. Primary crops grown here are potatoes, peas, lettuce, and cabbage. San Luis currently has a population of about 800 people. The town features adobe architecture and has a 600-acre shared crop-growing area. It is the county seat of Costilla County and is located about thirty-five miles southeast of Alamosa at the foot of Culebra Peak near the mouth of the San Luis Valley. A recent decision of the Colorado Supreme Court has restored the grazing and firewood gathering rights of the descendents of the early Hispano settlers. They are now allowed to use the slopes of the Sangre de Cristo Mountains outside San Luis for these activities.

Several books have been written about the unusual recent happenings in the San Luis Valley. Odd things are often reported in the night sky such as flying bubbles, black helicopters, and strange lights. Sometimes residents report eerie sounds coming from beneath the ground. The eastern parts of the valley have been declared an official Military Operations Area (MOA) by Congress. Some people think that the UFOs reported by some observers are really some type of secret military aircraft

Juan de Ulibarri and Pedro Villasur

In the late 1600s, a group of Picurie Indians left Taos, New Mexico. They may have been kidnapped by the Apache or they may have been slaves who were trying to get away from Spanish rule and therefore went with the Apache willingly. But in 1706, the governor received word that the Picurie wanted to return, and he sent Juan de Ulibarri to bring them back.

Ulibarri went north from Santa Fe to Taos with a force of soldiers, settlers, and Native Americans. He went as far as present-day Trinidad and crossed the Purgatoire River. He reached the Arkansas River near present-day Pueblo, Colorado. Twenty days after leaving Santa Fe, Ulibarri reached the Picurie Indians with the Cuartelijo Apache in eastern Colorado. He brought them back to Taos. During this trip, Ulibarri claimed the land in Colorado for Spain.

In 1720, Pedro Villasur led a group of men north. They probably went over Raton Pass to the Platte River. He was looking for French soldiers, because the Spanish feared that the French might try to claim this area. Villasur's fears were well founded. He and his men were killed by a group of French and Native Americans.

Don Juan Maria Rivera was another early explorer. In 1761, he led the first of three groups into the San Juan area. In 1765 he reached the spot where the Uncompahgre and Gunnison Rivers meet. In the La Plata Mountains he and his group found silver, but there is no record that the Spanish did much mining in Colorado.

Father Escalante and Father Dominguez, Catholic priests, explored Colorado in 1776. They were looking for a way to California from Santa Fe. They wanted to find a route north of the hostile Native Americans and establish a trail that would avoid the deserts and canyons of Arizona.

Father Escalante entered Colorado near Pagosa Junction. His group went around the San Juan Mountains and followed the San Miguel River upstream. Then they went down the Uncompahgre River to Gunnison. Near Gunnison, Father Escalante got two Native American guides who led the group across Grand Mesa to the Colorado River. They went north to the White River and followed it into Utah where the wild canyon country caused Father Escalante to give up his search. He and his men returned to New Mexico. The group had spent five months and traveled about 1,800 miles.

Father Escalante kept a detailed journal of his travels describing the rivers and mountains. This journal allowed the first maps to be drawn of the area.

Anza and Chief Greenhorn

Juan Bautista de Anza joined the Spanish militia in Mexico in 1751 and rose through the ranks to become an army captain. He got permission from the viceroy to lead a small group of men to try to find a route from Mexico to Alta, California. He succeeded in reaching the coast in seventy-four days, becoming the first European to establish an overland route from Mexico, through the Sonoran Desert, to the Pacific coast of California. Then in 1775, he led a large group of men, women, and children over much of the same route to colonize what is now the San Francisco Bay area.

From 1777 until 1787, Juan Bautista de Anza served as the

king of Spain's colonial governor of New Mexico. At this time, New Mexico included land that is now part of southern Colorado.

In 1779, Anza set out on a special assignment. The Comanche were a powerful Native American group and were often called "Kings of the Plains." One group of the Comanche was led by a chief that the Spanish called Chief Cuerno Verde, or Chief Greenhorn. They gave the chief this name because he often wore a headdress that included green-tinted buffalo horns. Chief Greenhorn kept attacking Spanish settlements such as Taos in New Mexico.

Anza set out with his men to find Chief Greenhorn. Both Anza and Chief Greenhorn were considered clever and fierce fighters, and it is possible that each was seeking some sort of revenge. Greenhorn's father had been killed during a raid on the Spanish and Anza's father was killed by the Apache when Anza was a small child.

Anza's journey to track down Chief Greenhorn would take him an estimated 615 miles in twenty-six days on horseback. Anza led several hundred soldiers who were joined by a group of Ute. They were led by Ute and Apache scouts. During the trip, Anza crossed Poncha Pass into the Arkansas Valley of Colorado.

Anza took a route that others had not tried. He was going to approach the Comanche from the north. Hoping to surprise the Comanche, he sometimes traveled at night when it would be hard to see the army moving. Anza kept a detailed account of his expedition. Once, crossing South Park, they came upon a herd of buffalo and killed and dressed fifty of these for food for the men. Then Anza continued eastward, probably crossing to the south of Pikes Peak.

Finally, Anza and his men came upon a small band of the Comanche. The soldiers quickly attacked, killing and capturing the Native Americans. From their prisoners, the soldiers learned that this very camp was to be the meeting place where Chief Greenhorn was expected to return from a recent raid to Santa Fe.

Anza and his men camped near Fountain Creek and waited. Soon Chief Greenhorn arrived. The final battle is thought to have taken place about eighteen miles south of Pueblo. During the battle, Chief Greenhorn as well as his son, his second in command,

Jumping Eagle, and his medicine man were killed. Many of the other captured Comanche were released.

A formal peace treaty with all three Comanche bands was finally signed in 1786. Greenhorn Valley and Greenhorn Peak were named after the Comanche chief.

In 1787, the Spanish tried to get the Comanche to live and farm in an area that is now the city of Pueblo. But the Comanche did not like this way of life, and they left the following year, moving eastward.

Important Changes

The coming of the Spanish made a big difference in the lives of the Native Americans in Colorado and the American Southwest. One of the most important changes was introducing them to horses. Once the Native Americans had these animals, their way of hunting and living altered greatly.

After Mexico won its war and became free of Spain in 1821, rights to the Colorado–New Mexico lands went to Mexico. This brought an end to the exploration of the American Southwest by Spain.

The Mexican government began giving large pieces of land to people who wanted to homestead and settle the new lands. But more often than not, these early colonists were killed or driven out by Indian attacks. It was not until the 1850s that the villages in this vast new area really began to take hold, and Colorado finally had permanent settlements.

Activities for Further Exploration

1. Coronado was an interesting explorer. You might want to see what route he followed in Colorado. One very useful Internet site is http://southwest.library.arizona.edu/jour/front.1_div.4.html. To read more about Francesco Vasquez de Coronado, see his picture, and learn about his life and travels, visit http://www.desertusa.com/mag98/sep/papr/coronado.html.

2. Many place names in Colorado are Spanish. When you see or hear these names, you could use a Spanish/English dictionary to find out what they mean. For example, La Plata Mountains means the Silver Mountains. You might want to write these names and their meanings on cards and collect them. As you study more about Colorado, your collection of Spanish names and their meanings will grow.

3. Father Escalante and Father Dominguez made a famous expedition that took them through land that is now the state of Colorado. Learn more about their journeys. An Internet site that will provide information and a map of the journey is at http://history forkids.utah.gov/history_and_facts/explorersandtrappers.html.

4. Mexico won its independence from Spain, and this had some direct effects on Colorado history. You might want to learn a little more about this event and the holiday that is celebrated around it. A useful resource book is *Mexican Independence Day and Cinco de Mayo* by Dianne M. MacMillan.

Chapter 6
Explorers, Trappers, and Traders

The people who had emigrated from Europe to make their new homes on the East Coast of America didn't think much about the Far West. They were much too busy settling a new land. But over time, a few people slowly moved inland. Then President Thomas Jefferson bought a large piece of land from France in 1803. This was called the Louisiana Purchase. The Louisiana Purchase almost doubled the size of the United States.

The United States paid $15 million for 828,000 square miles of land. The Louisiana Purchase included everything west from the Mississippi River to the Rocky Mountains and from the Gulf of Mexico to the Canadian border. Thirteen of the United States were later created from this land.

Zebulon Pike—Lost Explorer or Spy?

One of the early explorers of the land known as the Louisiana Purchase was Lieutenant Zebulon Pike. In 1805, Pike commanded a twenty-man exploring party to search for the headwaters of the Mississippi River as well as to check on the British fur trade and to negotiate treaties with Native Americans. Although on this expedition Pike did not convince any chief to come with him back to St. Louis, he did arrange to purchase land from the Dakota Indians that was later used to build Fort Snelling.

Pike and his men traveled by keelboat up the Mississippi from St. Louis to Prairie du Chien in what is now Wisconsin, and from there went by dugout canoes and finally on foot covering 2,000 miles on their journey to northern Minnesota. Pike and his men met and were the guests of the Englishman in charge of the North West Trading Post at Cedar Lake. This journey of exploration took Pike eight months and twenty-two days.

Only two months after he returned from this strenuous trip, in 1806, General James Wilkinson sent him out again. This time he went to explore the western lands around the Red River and the

Arkansas River. While on this mission, with about two dozen men, Pike traveled the Missouri and Osage Rivers. After they crossed Kansas, Pike explored Colorado. He led his men up the Arkansas River. They camped at the foot of a very high mountain and tried to climb it. Heavy snows turned them back, and Pike is said to have claimed that this peak was so high it might never be climbed. Later this mountain would be called Pikes Peak.

Pike continued exploring the Arkansas River. He went into South Park and across the hills near Trout Creek Pass. During the winter, he and his men crossed the Sangre de Cristos where they spent several desperate days in the deep snow fearing that they might freeze to death. They continued all the way to the foot of the White Mountains until they sighted the Great Sand Dunes.

Pike then journeyed into New Mexico, which was then owned by Spain. While he camped near the Rio Grande, he and his men were taken into custody by the Spanish who correctly argued that in coming there, Pike was trespassing on Spanish land.

Great Sand Dunes.

Pike insisted that he was lost. He said that he thought the Rio Grande River was the Red River. According to some historians, this might be true. Pike had been lost more than once before. Others think that Pike deliberately crossed into Spanish territory and wanted to be taken prisoner by the Spanish. In this way, he could see the Spanish lands up close and note where their forts and villages were located. Then he could report this information back to General James Wilkinson. Those who favor this version of the story believe that Wilkinson and Vice President Aaron Burr wanted to separate the western half of the United States and make it a separate country.

Whether he was lost or whether he was there as a spy, Pike was taken as a prisoner by the Spanish to Santa Fe and then to Chihuahua. He was taken across Texas and finally released at the Spanish-American border in Louisiana. The Spanish insisted on an apology for what they considered Pike's trespass on their land. The U.S. government refused to apologize and said that Pike was simply lost. As a result, diplomatic relations between the two countries were broken off.

During the War of 1812, now at the rank of a brigadier general, Pike lead 1,700 men in an assault on York (Toronto) in Canada. The troops were ferried across Lake Ontario. The British constructed and concealed a huge explosive mine. When it was set off, Pike was killed at age thirty-four by a heavy rock thrown up by the land mine.

Pikes Peak.

During all these adventures, Pike kept notes and a diary. After he was arrested at the Rio Grande River, he had to turn over his notes and papers to the Spanish, but he was able to hide and keep his diary. In it he described much of Colorado including the Royal Gorge, South Park, and the Upper Arkansas Valley. Pike told about the majestic mountains he had seen and the Native Americans he had met. He compared the vast plains of America to the deserts of Africa, and he described in detail the Spanish lands of New Mexico.

The Long Expedition

Stephen H. Long came to Colorado in the summer of 1819. His scientific expedition included a naturalist, zoologist, and a physician who was knowledgeable in both geology and botany. Dr. Edwin James kept a detailed diary of their trip as they explored the Platte, Arkansas, and Red Rivers. Members of the group also made drawings and paintings and collected plant specimens.

It was hot when Long and his group of twenty-two men, including two French guides, crossed the plains. The grasslands were dry and, in some places, sand had piled up. On his map, Long labeled these thousands of square miles as the "Great Desert." Then he followed the Platte River to the base of the mountains. Longs Peak in Colorado is named after him. Three men in his party, including Dr. Edwin James, climbed Pikes Peak.

Longs Peak.

At one point, Long divided his men into two groups. While one group followed the Arkansas River, the other went looking for the Red River. But instead of finding the Red River, this group of men found and followed the Canadian River, exploring the Texas Panhandle.

When they returned East, people were eager to hear what Long and his men had seen. The reports of these early explorers about the "Great American Desert," high mountains, and Native

Americans discouraged some people from coming West. But a few were still interested. They thought it would be exciting to trade with the Native Americans, and they were eager to trap fur-bearing animals.

Throughout history, people have worn animal furs. Sometimes they wore furs simply for warmth. At other times, furs have been worn because it was fashionable. In England during the 1600s, hats made of beaver fur were very popular. For almost 200 years, beaver hats were worn by gentlemen. To supply the material to make the hats, ships brought beaver skins to England from America.

Trappers and Traders

Many beavers were trapped in the Rocky Mountains of Colorado. These fur trappers were often called "mountain men." They lived simply off the land. For food, they hunted deer and antelope. They dressed much like the Native Americans of the area, wearing moccasins and deerskin clothes. Mountain men hunted buffalo and wrapped themselves in buffalo robes when they went to sleep.

These trappers sometimes went alone and sometimes traveled in small groups. It was safer to be in a group in case they met unfriendly Native Americans. Trappers carried guns, along with flint to make a fire and lead to make bullets. They carried all the other necessary supplies in bags hanging from their saddle and usually had a pack animal for carrying traps, bed rolls, and small items to trade with the Native Americans.

In his journal, Zebulon Pike mentioned meeting mountain men in Colorado. Pike met James Purcell who trapped in the area from 1802 until 1805. Another early trapper was Ezekiel Williams, who entered the Colorado mountains from the north. In 1811 Williams trapped in the upper Arkansas Valley and South Park.

In 1822, William H. Ashley and Andrew Henry organized the Rocky Mountain Fur Company. They hired a group of mountain men to trap for them. One of these trappers was Kit Carson.

Kit Carson

Christopher Houston "Kit" Carson was born on Christmas Eve in 1809 in Kentucky. As a young boy he moved to Boone's Lick, Missouri, and grew up there. Kit Carson left home and joined a wagon train heading for Santa Fe, New Mexico, in 1826. Soon Carson was going on fur-trapping expeditions that took him from his home base in Taos, New Mexico, into the Rocky Mountains, and throughout the West. In the 1840s, Kit Carson worked as chief hunter at Bent's Fort. He kept the fort supplied with buffalo meat.

During this time, Carson lived among the Native Americans and learned to speak several of their languages. His first wife was an Arapaho and, after she died, he married a Cheyenne.

In 1842, Kit Carson became a guide for the explorer John C. Fremont and he led Fremont to Oregon, California, and through much of the central Rocky Mountains. Fremont liked his guide and included glowing reports about Carson in his writings about his explorations. These writings were published in Congress and appeared in newspapers all over the country. In this way, Kit Carson became famous.

At the end of the Mexican-American War in 1846, Kit Carson took up ranching in New Mexico. He drove his sheep to Sacramento, California, and sold them for a good profit at gold-rush prices.

For a time, Carson served as an Indian agent in New Mexico. He resigned this position to organize the New Mexico Volunteer Infantry during the Civil War. Although he had no formal military training, because of his skill and reputation, Kit Carson was commissioned as a colonel. Kit Carson's men fought in a Civil War battle at Valverde on the east bank of the Rio Grande. Carson's regiment turned back repeated Texas cavalry charges. As a result of his actions there, Kit Carson was promoted to brigadier general.

Kit Carson.
Courtesy of Denver Public Library,
Western History Collection, D.F. Barry,
B-695

The Confederates encouraged Indian hostilities as part of their war strategy against the U.S. government and Union Army. With this encouragement, the Navajo and Mescalero Indians raided New Mexico. Kit Carson was given the job of bringing these hostile Indians under control. First he went after a band of Mescalero Apache and succeeded in bringing 400 warriors and families to a reservation.

Then he was sent to Canyon de Chelly to bring the Navajo under control. Carson did not like this assignment and requested several times to be relieved of duty. He did not agree with the plan that said the Navajo had to surrender unconditionally or be killed. He sympathized with the fact that the Navajo did not want to be sent to a distant reservation by the government.

But Kit Carson followed orders. He marched through their territory destroying crops and livestock. In 1864, most of the Navajo surrendered. Kit Carson forced about 8,000 Navajo men, women, and children to walk 300 miles from Arizona to Fort Sumner, New Mexico. This came to be known as "The Long Walk."

After the Civil War, Kit Carson moved to Colorado. In 1866 he took command of Fort Garland and served for a year before retiring due to poor health. He died in 1868.

Trappers had to be skillful to find beavers. They traveled into the mountains looking for signs that beavers lived in the area. They might see beaver dams or sight the rounded dome of a beaver home sticking up in the middle of a pond. The door to a beaver home is hidden underwater. Sometimes the trappers saw stumps along a pond or stream. The trappers could tell that beavers had gnawed off small trees with their sharp, chisel-like teeth.

Mountain men trapped beavers in the fall and spring. Those trapped in the fall had thicker and glossier coats, which helped to protect them from the cold. Beaver trappers had their own ways of catching beaver. They would visit the beaver ponds to set their traps.

Trappers used special recipes to make up a mixture that had the smell of beaver in it, which they rubbed on a stick. They would put the stick through a trap and push it down into the shallow water with one end of the stick up out of the water. Beavers could smell the mixture on the stick and were fooled into thinking they could smell other beavers. If a beaver came over to the stick and stepped into the trap, it would be caught. The beaver would drown.

Beaver.

After setting traps in several places, the trapper would come back that way again in a day or two. He would check his traps, taking out the drowned beavers. Then he would move to a new spot and set more traps.

When the mountain men caught beavers, they would skin them on the spot and take their pelts back to camp. There the trappers dried the beaver skins. They stretched the skins over a frame made from a willow branch.

At the end of the trapping season, the furs were sent to market. Often they were shipped by way of the Missouri and the Platte Rivers to eastern cities. From there they were shipped to England. A good beaver pelt at that time would bring $6 to $8.

Rendezvous

Traders came to yearly trading fairs called rendezvous. They brought salt, sugar, blankets, tobacco, beads, and guns and traded these things for the beaver furs brought in by the Native Americans and the mountain men. Sometimes the trading went on in forts built just for this purpose, such as Bent's Fort and Fort Vasquez. Buffalo hides were also traded. The two important fur-trading companies were the American Fur Company and the Rocky Mountain Fur Company.

Bent's Fort courtyard, buffalo hide press.

Many of these early trappers and traders became famous. They include William Bent, Jim Baker, Lancaster Lupton, Jim Bridger, Thomas Fitzpatrick, Jedediah Smith, Uncle Dick Wootton, Louis Vasquez, Ceran St. Vrain, William Becknell, and Kit Carson.

Uncle Dick Wootton

Richens "Uncle Dick" Wootton lived from 1816 until 1893. Few people in the history of the West can claim to be as versatile as this man. Born and raised in Virginia, at the age of twenty he joined a wagon train headed for Bent's Fort in southeastern Colorado. There he joined up with other trappers and headed into the Rocky Mountains looking for furs.

In 1833, Wootton and nineteen fur trappers made one of the longest trapping expeditions ever recorded. It took these men two years to go up the Wind River Range into Wyoming, to Fort Vancouver in Washington, to Los Angeles, California, and back to Arizona and New Mexico.

Uncle Dick saw a lot of territory and made friends with the Arapaho who called him "Cut Hand," due to the fact that he was missing two fingers from his left hand.

Beaver trapping in Colorado was most important in the 1820s and 1830s. The need for beaver skins ended about 1840 when men stopped wearing beaver hats. They were no longer the fashion, and the price of beaver pelts dropped. Uncle Dick Wootton and other trappers had to find something else to do.

Uncle Dick scouted for the U.S. military during the Mexican War. Then he was employed by the Bent-St. Vrain Company in a kind of pony express. Wootten laid out the trail that went through Denver. He carried mail, money, and supplies between Fort St. Vrain and Bent's Fort.

Wootten also tried ranching near what is present-day Pueblo, Colorado. One of his most interesting enterprises was running a toll road. He constructed a twenty-seven-mile road with bridges over Raton Pass, connecting Trinidad, Colorado, with Raton, New Mexico.

And he charged people for traveling his road. His fee for a wagon was $1.50. Wootton was careful to always allow Native Americans to travel his road for free.

The early trappers and traders are a colorful part of Colorado history. But when their furs were no longer in demand, they changed with the times. Some turned to farming. Some became scouts for the army. Others became guides for the crowds of people who were beginning to move West.

Activities for Further Exploration

1. Write a story in which explorers, trappers, and traders talk about their daily activities as they sit around a campfire at night. Can you use all the information you have learned to make your campfire story authentic? Try your story out on a friend. One useful resource is http://hewit.unco.edu/dohist/trappers/themes.htm.

2. Make a model of Bent's Fort using cardboard shoe boxes, sticks, or clay. To make your model of the fort as accurate as possible, visit http://www.santafetrailscenicandhistoricbyway.org/bentof. html.

3. Other Colorado forts include Fort Lupton and Fort Vasquez. If you want to find out what these forts were like in the 1830s and what finally happened to them, two useful resources are http://stvrainsfort.homestead.com/history.html and http://www. coloradohistory.org/hist_sites/ft_vasquez/ft_vasquez.htm.

4. Beaver trapping allowed wealthy gentlemen to wear the popular beaver hats in England during the 1800s. Draw one of these fancy hats. For more information visit http://www.whiteoak. org./learning/furhat.shtml. To learn more about the daily life, work, and tools of trappers, see http://hewit.unco.edu/dohist/ trappers/trappers/themes.htm.

Chapter 7
Westward Movement

People had many reasons for leaving their quiet towns in the East to begin new lives in the Wild West. Some felt that by 1840, all the good land in the East had been claimed. So for some adventurous pioneers, it seemed that the only thing to do was to move West.

Although Colorado is located right in the middle of the country, the westward movement bypassed this area at first. Routes to California and Oregon went north and south of Colorado. Since early explorers described a "Great American Desert" in the central United States, the area didn't sound like an inviting spot to try to settle. People went around or through Colorado and kept going west.

Several routes led from the East to the West—none of them easy! You could go all of the way by sea by sailing from the East Coast around the continent of South America. Or you could go by a combination of sea and land travel. To do that, you sailed to Panama, traveled by land across the Isthmus of Panama, and then sailed again up the coast of Mexico to California. Or you could reach the Far West by going all the way by land following one of several overland trails.

Around the Horn

The journey from the East Coast to the West Coast by sea was long and difficult. One excellent written account, which is currently housed in the Museum of America and the Sea in Mystic, Connecticut, is that of Thomas Boyd. Between 1852 and 1854, Boyd, who had left Boston on a clipper ship, wrote letters to his two daughters describing his sea voyage.

Boyd points out in one of his letters to his children, "By looking at the atlas, you will see that we have to sail round the whole continent of South America to get to California by the sea." Boyd made his long voyage on the clipper ship *The Golden Fleece*. He made notes during his voyage and even drew maps and sketches. From Boston, he sailed along the entire coast of Brazil and Patagonia to Cape Horn, at the very tip of South America. Then he sailed west into the Pacific Ocean.

The distance might have been only 16,000 miles, but because of contrary winds and a zigzag course, Boyd estimated that the distance his ship actually traveled was closer to 20,000 miles. Boyd writes, "We had head winds a great deal of the time, a great many days of no wind at all, and sometimes blowing so hard and the sea so rough, we could not sail much."

Boyd observed that often the passengers did not know anyone on board, although sometimes fifty to 125 men from a mining company made up a group and traveled together. The cost was about $150 for a stateroom, five cubic feet of baggage space, and meals. At that time, this was a great deal of money.

His long journey from Boston to San Francisco took 142 days.

Discovery of Gold in California

Word quickly spread of the discovery of gold by James Marshall on John Sutter's land along the American River in California in January 1848. When gold fever struck, thousands headed to the West Coast. In 1849, about 80,000 men arrived in California. Only about half of these were American. Others came from Great Britain, Australia, Germany, France, Latin America, and China.

The same year that gold was discovered at Sutter's Mill, Mexico ceded California to the United States. In 1848, only about 14,000 Anglo and Hispanic people lived in California. By the next year, there were 100,000 people.

After California became a state in 1850, more and more people wanted to go there and they wanted to get there quickly. The journey around Cape Horn was too slow for many. In seeking a faster way to go, some gold seekers tried the combination sea and land route.

Across Panama

The shortcut by land across the Isthmus of Panama cut 8,000 miles off the journey from east to west by sea around Cape Horn. Some writers of the time made it sound as if a trip through the jungle between two stretches of ocean journey was an exotic adventure.

Bayard Taylor, a journalist, wrote, "The only sounds in that leafy wilderness were the chattering of monkeys as they cracked the palm nuts, and the scream of parrots, flying from tree to tree."

In fact, the journey across the isthmus was far from idyllic. Travelers got off their ship on the Caribbean coast near the mouth of the Chagres River, climbed into a *bungo*, a type of Panamanian canoe, and traveled the river for three or four days. If the river was high, the trip was dangerous and some *bungos* and passengers were lost. In the beginning, prices to travel in a canoe were cheap, about $5. But the natives quickly took advantage of the travelers and raised their prices to $25.

When the *bungos* landed, the weary travelers were still not at their destination. Another fifty miles of trail stretched ahead. Most people traveled this route on horse or mule, and they faced many dangers in crossing this stretch of jungle. Several travelers caught diseases including malaria, yellow fever, and cholera, and it became common for robberies to occur during any part of the passage across the isthmus.

Once in Panama City, the traveler might be lucky and get on a boat quickly. Other travelers might have to wait days or even weeks to catch a ship. Arrivals and departures of ships between Panama and San Francisco were undependable. Joseph Crackbon wrote an account of his trip from New York in which he states that he arrived at the mouth of the Chagres River on April 11, 1849. But he did not leave from Panama City for San Francisco until May 27, and he was not in the field digging for gold until September 11.

Eventually a railroad was built. The Panama Railroad ran from Aspinwall on the Gulf of Mexico to Panama City on the Pacific side. This was a distance of only forty-nine miles, but it took five years to build the tracks. After the railroad opened in January 1855, the trip across the isthmus became much simpler.

This way of getting from one coast to the other coast of the United States became very popular. Between 1848 and 1869, 375,000 people crossed the isthmus from the Atlantic to the Pacific, while 225,000 people crossed in the opposite direction.

Wagon Trains

While some people were using sea routes, many settlers made the journey from the East to the Far West by land. There was no transcontinental railroad at that time, so these people had to travel by horse, carts, wagons, or stagecoach. Many of these early pioneers came by wagon train.

A wagon called the Conestoga wagon had been built in Pennsylvania in 1725. In the East, people used these wagons to carry heavy goods across the mountains. Conestoga wagons were large and drawn by six horses. The bottoms of the wagons curved, rising at both ends. A hood made of canvas kept out sun, rain, and dust.

Prairie schooners were another kind of wagon. These were the wagons commonly used by people who came west. They were like Conestoga wagons, but smaller and lighter. They could be pulled by two to four horses or were sometimes pulled by oxen. Other pioneers came in ordinary farm wagons fitted with a top.

Wagon trains were simply a group of covered wagons that traveled together carrying people and supplies. Those who joined a wagon train drew up contracts. They elected officers for their group, decided the order of the wagons, and might hire guides. Each night, they drew their wagons together into a circle, with guards to keep watch while people and animals rested.

Only a handful of guides knew the way to the Far West. Maps were poor and there were few trails. It was safer to travel as part of a group in a wagon train because of the many dangers to face. Sometimes Native Americans attacked. Wagons broke down. People got caught in bad weather on high mountain passes. Food ran out. It is estimated that about one in fifteen people who tried to make the trip West died along the way.

Many western travelers began in Independence, Missouri. If they took the Santa Fe Trail, it was 780 miles from Independence to Santa Fe. People often got their wagons, teams, and other supplies in Independence and Westport, Missouri. Then they took the trail about 150 miles southwest to Council Grove, Kansas, a main point for groups of wagons to organize into a wagon train.

A wagon train going to Santa Fe would cross the Kansas plains to the Arkansas River. It would follow the river to its fork near Dodge City, Kansas. Those who took the north fork, called the Mountain Division, followed the river west to Bent's Fort in what is now Colorado. From there, they turned south, passed near Trinidad, Colorado, and went over Raton Pass.

Santa Fe Trail monument, Trinidad.

Those who took the south fork from Dodge City, Kansas, followed what was called the Cimarron, or Cutoff, Division of the Santa Fe Trail. This southern route was less rugged, but it was dry with poor grass and little wildlife. This trail crossed the Great Plains from the Arkansas River to Fort Union, New Mexico. Here the north and south forks of the Santa Fe Trail met.

The wagon trains usually went in early summer. The trip from Missouri to Santa Fe took forty to sixty days. People who were only trading and planning to return East would stay in Santa Fe for about a month. They sold manufactured goods for silver pesos. But while some people were traveling south into Santa Fe to sell goods, others were headed toward Oregon. These people were not trappers and traders. They wanted to find good farmland and settle down. A thousand pioneers set out for Oregon in 1843.

Some settlers took the trail from Independence to Santa Fe and then followed the Old Spanish Trail into Los Angeles, California. Others who set out from Independence, Missouri, took the Oregon-California Trail. These people went northwest to Fort Kearney on the south bank of the Platte River, which is located in south-central Nebraska.

From Fort Kearney the wagon trains went to Fort Laramie. Along the way they passed Chimney Rock in what is now Nebraska. Then they dodged mountain ranges until they reached Fort Hall, a fur post on the Snake River.

After reaching Fort Hall, those headed for Oregon traveled north on the Oregon Trail. Those who were headed for California traveled southwest on the California Trail and followed the Emigrant Trail in the Sierra Nevadas near what is now called Sonora Pass.

There were many variations on these trails. The journey to California or Oregon often took six months with covered wagons moving about two miles an hour. The wagon trains often stopped at military outposts, such as Fort Laramie. These outposts served as post offices, allowing passengers to drop off or receive mail.

In 1849, thousands of "49ers" made their way to California. Most of these gold seekers bypassed Colorado. The Oregon Trail ran through Wyoming, and so did the Central Overland Trail, which was a mail route to the coast.

Some emigrants did cross over northeastern Colorado. The Cherokee Trail was used in 1849 and crossed through Colorado to the California goldfields. From Pueblo, these gold seekers went to Fort St. Vrain on the South Platte River. They crossed the South Platte at the mouth of the Cache la Poudre, through the mountains toward Laramie Plains. This route ran west of what is present-day Fort Collins.

A second group of travelers came over the Cherokee Trail in 1850. They found a small amount of gold in Ralston Creek near what is now Arvada. A prospecting group led by William Green Russell began to search for gold in Colorado. They found some at Dry Creek south of Denver. This began the gold rush to Colorado.

The Smoky Hill Trail

It is estimated that 100,000 gold seekers set out for
Colorado in 1859. These westward travelers could follow
any one of several routes from St. Joseph or Kansas City,
Missouri, to Denver, Colorado. The safest route was to
take the South Platte Trail, which followed the old
Oregon Trail along the Platte River toward Julesburg.
Some took the Oregon Trail to Fort Laramie and then
went southward along the old Cherokee Trail east of the
mountains to Denver.

Unlike the California 49ers, the Colorado 59ers
were poorly equipped. They came in open wagons. Some
simply had pushcarts and wheelbarrows. Since they were
in a hurry, many took the fastest route to Colorado, which
was an old Indian trail across Kansas that followed the
Smoky Hill River.

In eastern Colorado, near present-day Limon, the
Smoky Hill Trail divided into three branches. The north
branch went through Arapahoe County. The south branch
went through Elizabeth and Kiowa. The middle branch
was the shortest route, so, of course, that was the way
everyone wanted to go. But this route had many problems.
Spring weather was often severe, and water was scarce for
animals and people. This stretch soon earned the name of
Starvation Trail.

Many who traveled the Smoky Hill Trail were
attacked by Native Americans. The rush of thousands of
people who created trails and settlements throughout the
middle of the country also led to killing and driving off
the area's great buffalo herds. In the early 1840s, it is estimated that 30 million buffalo roamed the western plains.
By the late 1860s, there were fewer than 15 million. By
1890, only about 500 buffalo were left. Clearly the inter-
ests of the American Indian groups who relied on these
hunting grounds and settlers swarming in to look for gold

or to settle and farm were in sharp conflict. Attacks by Native Americans on settlers increased.

The Smoky Hill Trail crossed Cheyenne County from east to west. John Fremont used this trail in his explorations as early as 1844. Many of the settlers who traveled this route to Colorado in 1859 painted on their canvas wagon covers, "Pikes Peak or Bust." But the hardships of the central fork, which was so treacherous that it was lined with abandoned property, broken wagons, dead horses, and many hastily dug unmarked graves, made many turn back. These returning wagons also had slogans painted on them, such as, "From Kansas and Starvation to Missouri and Salvation."

One account written by William R. Murphy, who began his trip on May 10, 1859, described how his party turned back when they realized that they did not have sufficient water. They rode back on their horses, leaving their wagons and all their possessions behind.

Fort Hayes was about halfway between Atkinson, Kansas, and Denver, Colorado. Originally called Fort Fletcher, Fort Hayes was an army post. It was active from 1865 until 1889 and provided protection to those who traveled the Smoky Hill Trail. In spite of the soldiers, travelers who used this route were often attacked by Southern Cheyenne and Southern Arapaho.

Stagecoach Days

In 1856, David Butterfield and his family journeyed West and settled in Kansas. Then he moved to Denver and opened a store in 1862. His wife and family joined him after a twenty-eight-day journey by ox wagon. Butterfield decided to establish the Butterfield's Overland Dispatch from Atchison via Topeka and the Smoky Hill Trail to Denver.

Butterfield's Overland Dispatch began carrying freight and

passengers from Kansas to Colorado using ox wagons sent in trains. These "Trains of the Plains" consisted of twenty-six wagons, covered in canvas, each drawn by three or more yoke of oxen.

By 1865 there was both an express and a stage line over the route. The first stagecoach over the "New Smoky Hill Route" arrived in Denver on September 23, 1865. The coach was met by a crowd of people waving flags and cheering. This stage line went 592 miles with relay stations about every twelve miles along the route. This stage ran, under three different owners, from 1865 until 1870.

Butterfield stagecoach.
Photo by Doug Hansen, courtesy of
Booth Western Art Museum,
Cartersville, GA

But although the stagecoaches were fast, they were not safe and easy. Many of these coaches were attacked by Native Americans. Harrowing stories exist of near-death escapes. The Native Americans also often destroyed stations along the route and drove off the stock. This stagecoach line was eventually replaced by the Kansas Pacific Railroad.

In spite of the dangers of travel, adventurous pioneers continued to press into Colorado. Ten years earlier, stories about the hardships and dangers of sailing around Cape Horn or crossing the Isthmus of Panama or being attacked by Native Americans on the plains did not stop the flood of gold seekers to California. And the tales of the many dangers on the overland routes, including the Smoky Hill Trail, did not stop the gold seekers from coming into Colorado.

Activities for Further Exploration

1. Use an outline map of the United States and mark on it the various wagon trail routes from east to west across the country. Draw in and label the various wagon trail routes using a key. For example, the route of the Santa Fe Trail might be drawn in red, while the Oregon Trail route is drawn in green. An interesting resource is *Facing West: A Story of the Oregon Trail* by Kathleen Kudlinski. To print out a detailed map of westward expansion between 1800 and 1835, visit http://www.lib.utexas.edu/maps/united_states/exploration_1820.jpg.

2. Can you imagine what it would have been like in the middle of the 1800s to make the journey from the East Coast to the West Coast by sailing around Cape Horn? Look on a map to see the distance you would need to travel. To read an account of what such a journey would be like, a useful information source is http://pbskids.org/wayback/goldrush/journey_capehorn.html.

3. Pioneers could take very little with them besides needed tools, food, and clothing when they journeyed west. Each family member could bring only a few treasures. Imagine that you are about to make such a trip. Make a list telling what special treasures you would take with you. A useful resource is *Adventures with the Santa Fe Trail: An Activity Book for Kids and Teachers* by Dave Webb.

4. Make a drawing of a typical prairie schooner wagon that pioneers took on their trek west. At http://www.endoftheoregontrail.org/wagons.html you'll find a detailed picture with parts labeled that you might want to print out. You can also find more useful information about wagon trains at http://library.thinkquest.org/6400/travel.htm.

Chapter 8
Early Gold, Silver, and Coal Mining in Colorado

The 49ers, rushing to the goldfields of California, ignored Colorado as they followed the various trails from Independence, Missouri, to the Far West. But when gold was found in Colorado ten years later, the 59ers came pouring into the state in search of gold and silver.

The Colorado Gold Rush

In 1858, the Russell brothers found gold along Cherry Creek and, by the end of that year, several hundred people hunting gold had arrived in Colorado. At first they lived in Denver and Auraria on each side of Cherry Creek. Then they spread out to other areas. Some of these gold seekers were lucky and struck it rich. George A. Jackson of Missouri made a strike at Chicago Creek. John Gregory of Georgia found gold in Gregory Gulch, and the community that grew up there came to be called Central City. In 1860, Abe Lee discovered rich gold diggings near what is now Leadville.

The first miners used picks, shovels, and even sticks. They dug in the ground to find "free" gold or nuggets and they also used pans to search for gold in the bottoms of streams. They would swish the water, sand, and gravel out of their pans, saving the heavy and valuable gold that sank to the bottom. Gold dust and gold nuggets were kept in a "poke," or small leather bag. Later, miners made sluice boxes, which worked something like a giant-sized gold pan. In a sluice, the gold sank to the bottom of the box, while the sand and gravel were washed away.

After free gold was gone, miners looked deeper for veins of gold. For this, they needed to use machinery. The gold that was still inside the mountains was called lode gold. Most lode gold was in quartz rock. Miners dug into the sides of mountains or dug deep into the ground to get out this rock. They chipped it out with picks and blasted it out with dynamite and lifted it out of the mine with a hoist. Machinery was used in a stamp mill to crush the rock so that the gold could be removed.

Mining companies began to grow. Ruins of these old mining sites in Colorado can be seen in such places as Idaho Springs, Georgetown, and Dumont.

Silver Heels

A small mining camp called Buckskin Joe with about 2,000 people grew up near what is now Alma, Colorado. It was established in 1859. The town had a cemetery called Buckskin Joe Cemetery. Today that cemetery is called the Alma Cemetery. It's located in a beautiful area that features a view of the mountains and aspen trees. Many of the graves in this cemetery are of people who died in a smallpox epidemic in 1861 and 1862.

Living there at the time of the epidemic was a dancer who entertained in the Buckskin Joe mining camp. She was known as Silver Heels. When smallpox struck, Silver Heels stayed to nurse the sick. According to the stories of the time, she nursed those who were ill and helped bury the dead in the cemetery. But after the epidemic, Silver Heels seems to have disappeared. Her own neat cabin was found to be empty.

Some people believed that Silver Heels fell victim to smallpox and her once beautiful face was terribly scarred, so she did not show herself again in the mining camp. There are stories of people who say they have seen a heavily veiled woman carrying flowers walking and weeping among the graves in the Alma Cemetery. But when anyone approaches, she seems to vanish into thin air. Some insist that this is the ghost of Silver Heels. A nearby mountain is named Mount Silver Heels in her honor.

These early miners worked hard, but often they took time out for fun. They sometimes held rock-drilling contests. Pairs of men would compete against other teams. One man would hold the drill and another would hit the drill with a hammer. The men worked fast in the hard rock, and in fifteen minutes a good team could drill three feet.

Miners tended to be superstitious, and many stories were told in and around the mines. For example, it was considered bad luck to let a woman go down in a mine. If miners thought that a mine had a ghost in it, they called the ghost a "Tommy Knocker." When there were unusual sounds or accidents, or when something strange happened in a mine, it was often blamed on the Tommy Knockers.

Although 1859 was the beginning of the gold rush in Colorado, all the gold strikes were not made at once. It wasn't until 1891 that the gold strike was made at Cripple Creek. The El Paso Mine there produced about $12 million in gold.

Instead of mining, some turned to other work. Many men worked in sawmills that grew up in every mining town. The lumber was used to build houses and stores but it was also needed for posts to keep the mine shafts from caving in.

Rocky Mountain Canaries

One of the most important animals to play a part in the opening of the West was the burro. Trappers and hunters needed animals to carry their supplies through the mountains. Burros hauled everything including food, guns, traps, blankets, and pelts.

Prunes monument, Fairplay.

Burros were also very important to the early miners. They hauled picks and shovels as well as the wood needed to build mine tunnels and tracks. The honking, braying, and squealing sounds of the burro was music that early miners liked to hear. So they gave their burros the nickname of "Rocky Mountain Canaries" in honor of their fine voices.

Two of the most famous burros lived in Fairplay, Colorado. One of these burros was named Prunes. He was born around 1867.

Prunes was owned by Rupert Sherwood. The burro became well known and loved by the people of Fairplay. Prunes was always carrying supplies in and out of town. After Prunes died in 1930, the people of Fairplay collected enough money to build a monument in memory of the beloved burro.

Rush to Silver

Not only was there a rush to mine gold, but there was also a rush for silver. In Leadville, gold was running out and people started to leave. Then, suddenly, silver was discovered there, and Leadville became a busy town again. In the Robert E. Lee Mine, $118,500 worth of silver was taken in a single day.

H. A. W. Tabor came to Colorado from Vermont. He was the postmaster at Oro City and also had a small store there. Two miners came to him needing food and supplies while they hunted for silver. He agreed to "grubstake" them. This meant that he gave them food, sometimes called grub. And in exchange for the grub, the miners agreed to give Tabor a part (stake) in any silver they found.

The two miners he grubstaked soon found silver at a mine known as the Little Pittsburgh. Because he had grubstaked them, Tabor was a one-third partner in all the silver they found. Tabor took the money he made from the Little Pittsburgh and bought the Matchless Mine in 1879 for $117,000. It was soon paying him

Matchless Mine, Leadville.

$80,000 to $100,000 a month. The same year that he bought the Matchless Mine, Tabor was elected lieutenant governor of Colorado. Tabor came to be known as the Silver King.

Shorty and Bum

Shorty the burro and Bum the dog are also remembered with a monument. This monument is on the corner of the Fairplay courthouse square. Shorty was born in Fairplay in 1906, and he got his name because of his very short legs.

horty and Bum memorial, Fairplay.

Shorty worked hard, but he had a bad habit. If anyone climbed on him, he would quickly buck that person off. Sometimes, just for fun, the miners tricked a newcomer. They would get the newcomer to climb up on the burro knowing what Shorty would do. Then the miners had the fun of watching as Shorty bucked the newcomer off his back.

By the time Fairplay's mines closed, Shorty was old and he was going blind. Shorty was left to graze by his owner. He was joined by a homeless dog named Bum. Each morning Bum would trot into town and Shorty would follow him. Bum would stop at the door of a house and Shorty would bray. Kind townspeople would come out of their homes to give the two animals biscuits and pancakes.

Bum would take care of Shorty first, because Shorty could hardly see. Bum would carry some food in his mouth to Shorty, and then he would go back and get more food for himself.

The custodian at Fairplay's courthouse let the two animals sleep in his garage during the cold winter months. In summer they would roam the hillsides near town. Bum was always careful to guide Shorty on the sidewalk where the dog and the blind burro were safe from cars. But in 1951, in two separate accidents, each animal was struck and killed by a car. Shorty was killed first. Bum died four months later. The people of Fairplay put up a stone marker in memory of the friendship of the two animals.

Baby Doe Tabor

Every Silver King needs a Silver Queen, and Baby Doe
Tabor became Colorado's Silver Queen. She was famous
for her beauty with her strawberry-blonde curls and deep-
blue eyes. She married Harry Doe, and
they moved to Central City to try their luck
at gold mining. Her husband fell into debt,
and Baby Doe sued for divorce on the
grounds of nonsupport. After her first mar-
riage to Harry Doe failed, Baby Doe
married H. A. W. Tabor.

Baby Doe Tabor.

Tabor had made a fortune with his
silver mines, especially on the Chrysolite
and Matchless Mines. He and Baby Doe
traveled widely, spent evenings at the Tabor
Grand Opera House, and gave expensive
parties. Baby Doe enjoyed jewelry, furs, and fancy gowns.
They had two daughters, nicknamed Lilly and Silver Dollar.

In 1893, the Silver Crash occurred when the U.S.
Treasury lowered the value of silver. Tabor lost his fortune, and he and Baby Doe and their daughters moved out
of their Capitol Hill mansion into a rented cottage. Tabor
took a job as Denver's postmaster, earning in a year what
he used to earn in a day.

Baby Doe Tabor lived in poverty for thirty-six years
after her husband died in 1899. To keep warm and dry, she
took to wrapping her feet and legs in gunnysacks tied with
string over her old boots. The Matchless Mine was lost to
foreclosure, but the owners of the mine gave Baby Doe
permission to live in the old supply cabin next to the shaft
house. She died there of a heart attack in 1935. Her frozen
body was found one day by her neighbors. This ended the
story of the Silver Queen, a woman who had risen from
rags to riches then fell back to rags again.

Silver strikes were made at Aspen in 1879. Five large mines had outlets on Aspen Mountain. One of the mines there is Aspen's Smuggler Mine. Finding pure "native silver" is rare, but occasionally nuggets were discovered in the silver mines around Aspen. In 1894, a 2,350 pound silver nugget was taken from the Smuggler Mine. It holds the world's record for the largest silver nugget ever found.

Silver strikes were made in other areas, too. The first silver strike in the Boulder Valley was in 1868. Sam Conger made the silver strike in the high country above Boulder near Nederland. By 1869 Caribou was a town, and by 1875 it had 5,000 people. After the Silver Crash of 1893 and a fire ten years later, the town of Caribou died.

Some methods of mining were expensive, and supplies of gold and silver eventually ran out. In 1958, Leadville produced a total of less than $200 worth of gold, silver, zinc, and lead. Many people quit mining. Some of the early famous mining towns are now ghost towns. Others survived. For example, many people still live in Leadville, but they no longer make a living by mining.

Coal Mining

Originally people came into the area around Trinidad on the Santa Fe Trail for cattle ranching and agriculture. But there were huge coal deposits beneath the hills and mountains of that area. Before long, coal miners went to work for the Colorado Fuel and Iron Corporation, and mining camps all along the river valley west of Trinidad were flourishing by 1905.

Most of these mining communities were company towns. This meant that the houses and stores were all owned by Colorado Fuel and Iron and the workers were paid in script, which was redeemable only at the company store. The men were paid low wages for their hard work. There were strikes in 1913 and 1914, culminating in the Ludlow Massacre in April 1914 when miners, women, and children were killed. (Discussed in Chapter 2 under Historic Sites.)

When news got out after the Ludlow Massacre, other miners were terribly angry and there was what amounted to a war. For ten days, miners attacked and destroyed mines and fought mine guards. The violence continued until the governor of Colorado asked President Wilson for troops to restore order.

There was a gradual decline in coal mining operations in Las Animas County from the 1930s until the 1960s until only the Allen Mine was working. Other parts of the state had working coal mines, too. The area around Boulder and Weld Counties once had more than 100 producing coal mines. Coal is still produced, primarily from open cut and underground mines, in north-western Colorado.

Coal Miners' memorial, Trinidad.

Present-Day Mining

Colorado not only has a rich mining history, but mining remains important in the state at the present time. Colorado's high-quality coal, for example, is still used to generate 82 percent of the electricity consumed in the state.

In addition to gold, silver, and coal, the following minerals are produced in significant amounts: lead, gypsum, limestone, molybdenum, uranium, and zinc. The Henderson Mine and Mill operated by Climax Molybdenum Corporation produced more than 21 million pounds of molybdenum valued at $55.5 million in 1999. And the Schwartzwalder Mine near Golden, Colorado, is the largest uranium mine in the United States.

Activities for Further Exploration

1. After you have read about being a gold prospector in Colorado, write a letter to a friend in which you pretend to be a gold prospector. Tell your friend about what you are doing, where you are living, and what tools and equipment you are using. See http://history.oldcolo.com/history/research/MINING1.html for background information. Make your letter as authentic as you can.

2. In learning about Colorado you will certainly read about H. A. W. Tabor and Baby Doe Tabor, who were the "king" and "queen" of silver. Photographs of both of them can be found at on the Web at http://www.babydoetabor.com. You might want to read *The Legend of Baby Doe: The Life & Times of the Silver Queen of the West* by John Burke, University of Nebraska Press.

3. If you have been adding names and places to the legend of your outline map of Colorado as suggested in the Introduction activities, be sure to add some of the famous gold and silver strikes to your notebook and map. Some of these early mining towns are now ghost towns. You might be able to visit the National Mining Hall of Fame & Museum in Leadville. You can read about mining camps such as Columbia City and St. Elmo at http://www.mining camps.com/columbia-city.htm.

4. Try writing an exciting mining story. Have some characters in your story come to town to get a merchant to grubstake them while they hunt for gold. Have the miners come back to town having struck it rich in a lucky strike. For reading about grub-staking in the town of Leadville, see http://www.leadville.org. Share your exciting story with a friend.

Chapter 9
Early Colorado Railroading

There were problems in building Colorado railroads. The many tall mountains in the state meant that finding and building train routes was difficult. And it was hard to convince people to invest their money in such projects. But some investors recognized the importance of transportation. They knew that trains were needed to carry ore from the mines, and they were also needed to carry passengers and freight. There was money to be made, so in the latter half of the 1800s construction of railroads in Colorado finally started.

The First Railroads in Colorado

Colorado was only a territory, not a state, when the first railroad came. This first transcontinental railroad was the Union Pacific. It crossed the northeastern corner of Colorado in 1869. The main line of the railroad came through Cheyenne, Wyoming.

Narrow gauge locomotive, Boulder.

The Denver Pacific was a branch line of the Union Pacific. This was the first railroad to reach Denver. The Denver to Cheyenne railroad was finished in June 1870. Just two months later, the Kansas Pacific Railroad came to Denver. And in another two months, the Denver and Rio Grande Railroad started up. Many other railroad companies were soon in Colorado. These early trains that puffed across the plains were often called Iron Horses.

But trains were needed to cross the mountains as well as the plains. This was a real challenge. Otto Mears and David Moffat were early railroaders in the Colorado mountains. David Moffat built the Denver, Northwestern, and Pacific Railroad. It crossed the

Continental Divide over Rollins Pass at Corona, which is 11,660 feet above sea level. Moffat dreamed of a time when men could tunnel right through the mountains, so that trains would not need to travel over high tracks where they might be trapped in snows. He died before the tunnel was built, but when the tunnel finally opened in 1928, it was named for him. The Moffat Tunnel still exists today near Rollinsville, Colorado.

In the mountains of Colorado, narrow gauge tracks were used for trains because they were cheaper to build. The rails of a narrow gauge track are only about three feet apart. The standard gauge tracks, which were used on the plains and for the transcontinental railroad, have about four feet between the rails.

The Denver and Rio Grande started in 1870. The leader in building this railroad was General William J. Palmer. Palmer was interested in building narrow gauge railroads in the mountains of Colorado. He knew that trains would make it possible to ship precious metals from the mountains and also help farmers and ranchers in the area by getting cattle and crops to market.

Otto Mears and Chief Ouray.
Courtesy of Denver Public Library,
Western History Collection,
William Henry Jackson, WHJ-10219

William J. Palmer—Railroader, General, and Union Spy

From his earliest youth, Palmer was interested in railroads. When he was seventeen, he went to work for the engineering corps of the Hempfield Railroad. That company sent him to England and France to study railroading. On his return, he became the private secretary to John Edgar Thompson, president of the Pennsylvania Railroad.

The Civil War began, and William Palmer wanted to be part of it. He raised and commanded the 15th Pennsylvania Cavalry in 1862. Shortly after the battle at Antietam, Palmer volunteered to go behind enemy lines to seek information on southern troop movements. When it became clear he was going to be captured, Palmer took off his uniform, put on civilian clothes, and tried to pass himself off as Mr. Peters. He hoped in this way to be released and to be able to return to the Union side with the information he had collected.

But he was not released. He was imprisoned for months as a civilian at Castle Thunder in Richmond, Virginia. He kept it a secret that he had been in the cavalry because if that were known, he would have been shot as a spy. When he was finally released in a prisoner exchange, he rejoined his regiment and distinguished himself in many campaigns. Palmer received the Medal of Honor and was promoted to brigadier general.

After the war he worked for the Kansas Pacific Railroad and then came to Colorado and started the Denver and Rio Grande Railroad. He helped lay out the plans for the city of Colorado Springs and built his first house there in August 1871. He reserved land and contributed funds to Colorado College, parks, and other worthy causes.

He built a sixty-seven-room Tudor-style castle, Glen Eyrie, in the rugged mountains near Colorado Springs on 700 acres. Today it is used as a resort and convention center.

The Rio Grande Railway

Since the Union Pacific Railroad had already been built east and west across the country, Palmer's dream was to build a north and south railway. He wanted to connect Denver with Mexico City. His new railroad would be built right through land that contained silver, gold, lead, copper, and iron. It would also tap fields of coal.

Palmer planned for the main line to go from Denver to Pueblo. Then it would go through the Royal Gorge to Salida, southward through Poncha Pass to Alamosa, and south to El Paso, Texas. Finally it would reach Mexico City. Palmer also planned for branch lines. One of these would connect Denver to Salt Lake City. This was a grand dream, but only a part of his dream ever came true.

Laying track for the Rio Grande Railway began in Denver on July 27, 1871. The first stretch was completed to Colorado Springs, seventy-five miles away, by October 21. Reports show that passenger traffic that first year between the two cities was about thirteen persons each way daily.

Rollins Pass railroad trestle.

The Denver and Rio Grande Railroad reached Pueblo in June of 1872. A branch line was also built in 1872 that went up the Arkansas Valley to the coalfields near Florence. These coalfields would provide fuel for the new railway.

In 1872, meetings were held with the Mexican government. This is when Palmer learned that part of his dream would never be realized. The Mexican government was not interested in having the Denver and Rio Grande Railroad extended to Mexico City.

Railroad Rivalries

Still, it was clear that railroads would be very important in the southern part of Colorado. More and more people were moving into the Arkansas Valley. The Atchison, Topeka, and Santa Fe

Railroad officials wanted to be part of this growth. They moved quickly to build their own railroad in southern Colorado.

These two railroad companies became rivals. The Denver and Rio Grande built a branch railway through La Veta Pass into San Luis Park. It reached Alamosa on July 6, 1878. The Rio Grande planned to construct a southern route through Trinidad, but the Santa Fe Railroad rushed men and work teams to Raton Pass, just south of Trinidad. Both of these companies eventually wanted to get the right-of-way through the Royal Gorge, which would be a route to the rich mining camps in the mountains.

Then, for a few years, almost all new railway construction stopped. The Panic of 1873 hit the United States, and money was scarce. The Panic of 1873 was a serious downturn in economics touched off by the bankruptcy of a large Philadelphia banking firm that had overextended its railroad financing. Of the country's 364 railroads, eighty-four went bankrupt, and a total of 18,000 businesses failed between 1873 and 1876. Fewer people rode passenger trains as the country sank into an economic depression. When money became plentiful again, work started on the new railways.

The Rio Grande put crews to work in 1878 on one of its branches through La Veta Pass into San Luis Park, while the Santa Fe rushed hundreds of men and teams to work in Raton Pass. The race was on. Which of the two companies would get the right-of-way through the Royal Gorge?

A huge argument broke out between the two railroad companies, and each took the other to court. Judges made rulings, but some of these rulings were changed by other judges, and the decisions made in one court were appealed in other courts. It looked as if the quarrel between these two railroad companies would never end. And this argument wasn't just fought in courtrooms. Men from both railroad companies got into fights with each other. Several people were killed in what might be considered a railroad war.

The Royal Gorge War

You might think that most of the gun fighting that went on in the West occurred during stagecoach and bank robberies or between settlers and Native Americans. But it turned out that railroad workers had their share of gun fighting, too. Many people said the battle between the Denver and Rio Grande Railroad and the Atchison, Topeka, and Santa Fe Railroad in southern Colorado was a war.

When Rio Grande railway men came to work in the mountains in 1878, they found armed guards at Raton Pass where Santa Fe railway men were busy grading. The next spring, both railways were building tracks to Leadville. The miners in that town were hauling up to 100,000 pounds of ore a day. Whichever railway carried this ore had a chance to be rich and successful.

Both the Santa Fe and the Rio Grande began laying tracks through the Grand Canyon of the Arkansas River. Each railroad caused as much trouble as it could for the other company's work crews. The Santa Fe brought in a well-known gunman named Bat Masterson who had worked as a deputy marshal for Wyatt Earp in Dodge City. On their side, the Rio Grande called in the state militia.

Hidden riflemen on both sides shot at work gangs. Each side burned bridges, moved survey stakes, and caused avalanches to impede the other. Tools left at work sites were mysteriously thrown into the river. Plots against each other were sent by telegraph with each side decoding the other's messages.

In the end there was a compromise. Because the whole thing had been like a war, some people refer to this court decision as the Treaty of Boston. The courts gave the Rio Grande the right to build to Leadville, and the Santa Fe got the exclusive railroad route into New Mexico. In time, the two railroads even worked together on a joint double-track system.

The agreement that was finally reached in the courts meant that the Rio Grande would never build its railway to El Paso, Texas. Nor would it build a line to St. Louis. But it did get to build the railway to Leadville, which it finally reached in July 1880. So instead of becoming a great north and south line as General Palmer had originally planned, the Denver and Rio Grande became an east and west line.

Extending Rail Lines

General Palmer bought the Pleasant Valley Railway of Utah. Under the name of the Rio Grande Western Railroad, it was extended to the Colorado line. This made a narrow gauge line from Denver to Salt Lake City and to Ogden, Utah. And within the next few years, a third rail was laid. Finally, a standard gauge line ran between Denver and Pueblo and a standard gauge line connected Denver to Ogden.

The Denver, South Park, and Pacific Railway was another early narrow gauge line in Colorado. It began in 1872 and changed names and ownership a number of times. It started in Denver and followed the South Platte River through Englewood, Waterton, and then to South Platte. Leaving the river at that point, it headed west. It went through several small towns, over Kenosha Pass, and into South Park. It passed through Jefferson and into Como. There the route split. One route went south, while the other went northwest over Boreas Pass and into Breckenridge.

The Colorado Midland Railway was incorporated in 1883. Its plan was to build a railway and telegraph line from Colorado Springs through the Ute Pass into South Park. From there it would go to Salida and Leadville. Later they planned to add branch lines to Fairplay, Alma, and Aspen.

The Denver and Rio Grande Railway and the Union Pacific Railway didn't want to compete with yet another railway. They raised freight prices, which made it hard for the new railroad to get needed construction materials. But work began on the Colorado Midland in 1886. The first regular train service began in July 1887 after the railroad reached Buena Vista. The new railroad offered both passenger and freight service.

On August 31, 1887, tracks were laid into Leadville, and by November, the tracks reached Basalt. One group continued to work on the Aspen branch while the other group built track to Glenwood Springs. The railroad reached Glenwood Springs on December 18, 1887, and trains reached Aspen on February 4, 1888.

By 1899, a network of railroads crisscrossed Colorado. The Denver and Rio Grande built a new standard gauge line to Alamosa. They replaced the early narrow gauge line that had been built across the Sangre de Cristo Range in 1877, but the Denver and Rio Grande continued to operate many narrow gauge lines in the southwestern part of the state. These mainly served mines and sawmills. Several small narrow gauge railroads were also built into the mountains west of Boulder along what was called the Switzerland Trail.

Rio Grande locomotive.

The Colorado and Southern included a standard gauge main line that went from Fort Collins, Colorado, to Texline, Texas. The Union Pacific, Chicago Burlington and Quincy, Chicago Rock Island and Pacific, Missouri Pacific, and the Atchison, Topeka, and Santa Fe all entered Colorado from the east. Except for the Santa Fe line, they all ended at the foot of the mountains.

The Colorado Fuel and Iron Company was a small steelmaker and coal and coke producer. In 1899, it grew through an arrangement with eastern steelmakers and began to make and ship badly needed steel rails.

The Colorado Fuel and Iron Company searched for new iron deposits and developed properties in Colorado, New Mexico, Wyoming, and Utah, using many spur and branch railroads. As the

Blizzard on the Train Tracks

In 1883, the Colorado Midland Railway Company was incorporated to construct and operate a railway from Colorado Springs into South Park and then to Salida and Leadville with a branch to Fairplay and Alma. Two years later James Hagerman became president of the Midland Railway Company and tried to turn the plans on paper into real train tracks.

In the spring of 1886, more than a thousand men were hacking a grade at Hagerman Pass and boring a 2,161-foot tunnel. It was considered a great engineering feat when it was completed, and passenger and freight trains began running through this tunnel. But this track, which was located at 11,528 feet elevation, was hard to keep clear of snow in winter, and it was expensive to run.

After the company was sold in September 1890 to the Santa Fe Railroad, the new management decided to build a new train tunnel at a lower elevation. Work began on the Busk-Ivanhoe Tunnel, which was fifteen feet wide, twenty-one feet high, and more than 9,000 feet long. It took three years to complete the new tunnel and, when it was finished, use of the old loop tunnel over Hagerman Pass was suspended in 1894.

The new Busk-Ivanhoe Tunnel had a west portal 133 feet higher than its east portal. It was thought this difference would cause the tunnel to act something like a chimney to exhaust the tunnel of engine fumes. Problems became evident immediately. Once a train engine went through, it took forty minutes for the smoke and gas to clear out of the tunnel.

After the railroad went bankrupt and reorganized, the new railroad officials decided to reopen the old loop line through Hagerman Tunnel. The trains used this tunnel in 1897 and 1898. But on January 21, 1899, a huge storm hit the area. A stock train with three engines started through the tunnel and down the east side. They reached a snow shed that had collapsed onto the tracks under the heavy load of snow. By this time, the track behind them had drifted shut. They were trapped.

Plows were brought in to try to reach the stranded train. These plows would make progress in clearing the tracks, and then another blizzard would strike and undo all their earlier efforts. Storms and one problem after another delayed the rescue. A passenger train also caught in the storm managed to return to Busk after a plow freed it, and the train backed down the hill, turned, and returned to Leadville. It took seventy-eight days to clear the tracks. The load of cattle trapped on the train during the storm froze to death and when plows finally opened the track, the lifeless stock was pulled to Busk. The old loop through Hagerman Tunnel was closed for good in the autumn of 1899.

company grew, it needed its own transportation department. Work began on building the Southern Division of the Colorado and Wyoming Railway on December 23, 1900.

The starting point of the new railway was about two miles west of Trinidad on the Atchison, Topeka, and Santa Fe Railroad. A yard and roundhouse were built at this junction, which was named Jansen. The railroad followed the canyon of the Purgatoire River. The track reached Segunda at the mouth of Smith's Canyon. The railroad was open to the Primero Mine there in 1901. Primero grew to be one of the largest coal mines in the West, producing 65,000 tons a month.

Hundreds of people came to the area to work for the railroads and the coal mines, and coke ovens were built nearby. The Colorado Fuel and Iron Company had thirty-eight mining and coke camps in Colorado, Utah, New Mexico, and Wyoming. Many of their employees were recent immigrants to this country.

The Colorado and Wyoming Railroad also kept busy. Nine locomotives and thirty-five train crews worked on the Southern Division pulling loads of slack coal for the coke ovens and pulling coal and coke to Jansen. Inbound freight included timber and machinery and goods for the mining camps.

The Northern Division of the Colorado and Wyoming Railroad was a short line used to transport raw materials. The Middle Division of the railway lay almost completely within the Colorado Fuel and Iron Company's steel mill in Pueblo.

In the early part of the 1900s, railways in the United States generally declined. Passengers started using trolleys, buses, and autos. A lot of freight went by trucks. Planes carried mail and packages. Only time will tell if passenger and freight trains become popular again.

A few special train rides are still available in Colorado to give visitors the flavor of early railroads. One is a narrow gauge trip that runs from Durango to Silverton. The city of Durango was founded in 1879 by the Denver and Rio Grande Railroad. The railroad arrived in Durango in 1881 and was completed to Silverton in 1882.

It hauled gold and silver from the San Juan Mountains.

Today the Durango to Silverton trains run mainly for tourists and operate during the summer months. The trains are pulled by steam engines. Passengers may ride in an open or closed coach. These trains use cars that may have been built as early as 1879 or as late as 1964. The interiors of the older cars look much as they did in the 1880s except for replaced carpet and seats.

Fishermen and hikers can get on and off of this train at several flag stops along the way as the train travels along more than forty-five miles of railroad track. The route follows the Animas River out of Durango and ends in Silverton at an elevation of 9,288 feet.

The early railroads opened up the West and united the country. In the last half of the 1800s, one railway after another was built, and a few of these railways are still in operation.

Activities for Further Exploration

1. Driving the golden spike that completed the railroad track that tied the eastern and western United States together was a big moment in America's history. If you want to find out more about this event, a useful Internet resource for data on the transcontinental railroad is http://usparks.about.com/library/weekly/aa121704.htm. For an interesting book, see *Full Steam Ahead: The Race to Build a Transcontinental Railroad* (National Geographic, 1996) by Rhoda Blumberg.

2. Even with automobiles and airplanes, railroads still play an important role in the United States. Do you know which passenger and freight trains still run through Colorado? You might enjoy reading *All Aboard! A True Train Story* by Susan Kuklin.

3. Many famous ballads are sung about work on the railroads. Can you locate some records, tapes, or CDs of these? Perhaps you can learn to sing a few. A useful resource is *A Treasury of Railroad Folklore: The Stories, Tall Tales, Traditional Ballads, and Songs of the American Railroad Man* by Benjamin Albert Botkin.

4. John Henry was a famous railroad folk hero. You might enjoy reading *John Henry* by Julian Lester with drawings by Jerry Pinkney (New York: Dial, 1994) or watching the video recording *Disney's American Legends*, Walt Disney Home videos, 58 minutes, narrating four short stories including one on John Henry.

Chapter 10
Farming and Ranching in Colorado

As the state of Colorado grew and changed, so did its economy. More than 4 million people currently live in the state, and the Colorado labor force is made up of 2.3 million workers. Manufacturing, tourism, mining, and many businesses and industries involving high technology are important parts of the state's economy.

But even with new high-tech industries, farming and ranching, which were tremendously important in the state's early history, remain important today. At the beginning of the twenty-first century, nearly half of Colorado's 66 million acres are being used for

agriculture. There are about 29,000 farms and ranches in the state. These farms and ranches add more than $12 billion to Colorado's economy every year and provide 86,000 jobs.

Counted in millions of dollars brought into the state, the top farm and ranch products for Colorado in 2001 were

Farm, Boulder County.

cattle, corn, wheat, and vegetables. Colorado is also a large producer of dairy products, hay, hogs, poultry, and eggs. Colorado ranks fourth among states in the production of all sheep and lambs. Some sheep are raised just for their wool, but in northern Colorado and in the Arkansas Valley, lambs are fattened for the market.

Colorado farmers and ranchers help feed the world. The state exports more than $1 billion worth of farm and ranch goods annually. The biggest overseas buyers of Colorado foods are Japan, Korea, Mexico, and Canada.

Early History

Some of the early explorers in Colorado were trappers and traders. These men were soon followed by gold seekers. The big influx of people hunting for gold in Colorado created a market for meat, flour, fruits, and vegetables. To some, the life of a rancher or farmer was more appealing than prospecting for gold. So Colorado's agricultural industry began right on the heels of the gold rush.

Ranching

Early Colorado ranchers raised cattle, sheep, hogs, chickens, and turkeys, with the main focus on cattle. Cowboys drove Texas longhorns up to graze on Colorado's plains in the 1860s.

Cattle ranch, Weld County.

Trail drives were very common from the end of the Civil War until the mid-1880s. Cowhands rode long distances driving the cattle from grasslands to centers where they could be taken to market. An outfit for a typical trail drive consisted of a boss, ten to fifteen cowboys, each of whom had a string of five to ten horses, a horse wrangler (*remudero*), who drove the cow horses, and a cook.

On the early long-trail drives, cowboys had to make do with what they could carry. Then in 1866, a Texas rancher named Charles Goodnight outfitted the first chuckwagon. Several other manufacturers followed. Cowboys were a lot more comfortable after they were provided with a cook and chuckwagon to provide hot meals and to carry supplies.

The chuck box added to the rear of a wagon had shelves and drawers to hold everything that a cook needed. One hinged lid dropped down to serve as a work surface. The wagon boot carried

Dutch ovens and other cooking utensils that were needed to provide hot meals for ten or more cowboys.

A water barrel large enough for two days' worth of water supply was attached to the side of the wagon along with other needed tools and a coffee grinder.

Canvas was suspended beneath the wagon like a hammock to hold any fuel that was collected along the day's trip, since wood was often scarce. A wagon box that was ten feet long and about forty inches wide carried the cowboys' bedrolls and personal effects. It

Chuckwagon at Iliff Ranch,

also carried bulk food and feed for the horses. Sometimes a second wagon, called a hoodlum, was needed to carry all the supplies for a large crew.

From the mid-1860s until the late 1880s, cattle were left alone most of the year to graze on what was called open range. These cattle wandered and ate grass where they wanted. During winter, herds drifted about a good distance and got mixed up with other animals. So in spring there was a roundup. Cowboys would round up all the cattle bearing their ranch brands. They would gather the calves, too, and brand them.

Branding

Branding, or permanently marking animals with a hot iron, has a long history. More than 4,000 years ago, a branding scene was drawn on an Egyptian pyramid. It is thought that Hernando Cortez introduced branding from Spain to the New World in 1541. Branding was used in the Colorado Territory beginning in 1866.

More than 38,000 different brands are now registered in the state of Colorado with the Colorado Cattlemen's Association. In the spring after calving and again in the fall after roundup, cattle are brought to their home ranch. Most newly born calves are branded in the spring, while any calves born in summer or missed in the spring are branded in the fall roundup.

Traditionally, calves are roped from horseback and then a branding iron made of iron or steel is heated to the color of gray ashes in an open fire. The hot iron is applied for three to five seconds to burn the hair follicles of the calf without burning through the hide. The scar that is left is called a brand. At this same time, cattle may receive ear marking for identification and vaccinations against diseases. These and other procedures are done in succession by a team of men.

Brands are composed of capital letters of the alphabet, numerals, pictures, and characters such as a slash, circle, half-circle, cross, or bar. A part of the brand can be upright, lazy (lying down), connected, combined, or reversed. Brands, just like words on pages in a book, are read from top to bottom and left to right. Two ranchers might use the same brand if it was applied to a different area of the animal.

Typical Brand Designs

Spanish Mission Brands

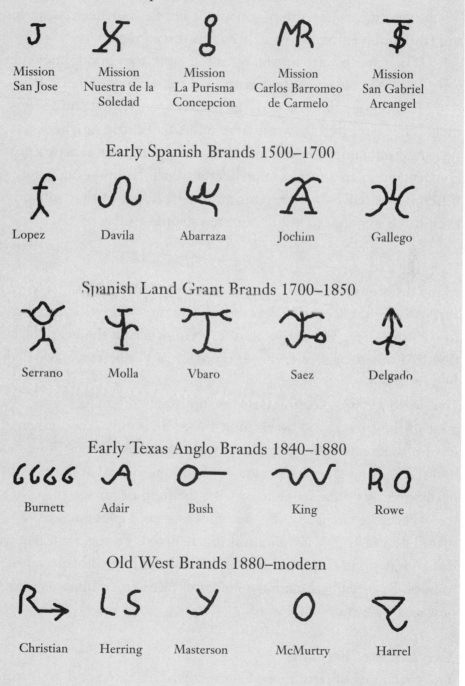

Mission San Jose

Mission Nuestra de la Soledad

Mission La Purisma Concepcion

Mission Carlos Barromeo de Carmelo

Mission San Gabriel Arcangel

Early Spanish Brands 1500–1700

Lopez

Davila

Abarraza

Jochim

Gallego

Spanish Land Grant Brands 1700–1850

Serrano

Molla

Vbaro

Saez

Delgado

Early Texas Anglo Brands 1840–1880

Burnett

Adair

Bush

King

Rowe

Old West Brands 1880–modern

Christian

Herring

Masterson

McMurtry

Harrel

Each fall, cowboys would round up their cattle and drive them to railroad stations where they were loaded on cattle cars and sent to eastern slaughterhouses. By 1882, grasslands were overstocked. Then two disastrous winters wiped out herds. Ranchers began fencing land and feeding their cattle hay in the winter.

Then sheep were moved onto the land, too. Sometimes there were battles between cattlemen and sheepmen over grazing lands.

Range wars didn't just occur between cattlemen and sheepmen. They occurred between large and small cattle ranchers, too. As rangeland and water became scarcer, barbed-wire fences were constructed in an attempt to protect water holes and rangeland. Often, these fences were mysteriously cut. Large cattle companies even hired gunmen to kill or frighten people away.

Farming

Many different kinds of crops are raised on farms in Colorado. This variety of crops is possible because of the great variation in elevation in the state. The five counties in Colorado in the year 2001 that had the greatest value from crops were Weld, Yuma, Morgan, Logan, and Kit Carson.

Although pioneering farmers and ranchers in Colorado raised a lot of their own food by keeping a garden, a milk cow, and chickens for meat and eggs, they also bought supplies such as flour, salt, and spices from stores. Farmers worked long hours, and most of the hard work was done by hand or with the help of horses and mules.

Farming changed over the years as new implements were made. By the 1870s, farming was mechanized. Farmers cut hay with horse-drawn mowing machines and baled the hay with special hay presses. Eventually these huge pieces of farming equipment were powered by motors instead of horses.

Two Kinds of Farming

The two kinds of farming in Colorado are irrigated and dry farming. Irrigated farms receive regular watering through canals and sprinkler systems. Dry farming simply depends on rain. Most farm

Range Wars

Cattlemen in Colorado loved what seemed to them to be the endless range of grass that was available for cattle grazing. George and Charles Woolley, who were pioneers in Routt County, were typical of early cattlemen. They arrived in 1893 and bought 320 acres on the Yampa River east of Craig. Soon they added another 200 acres, and they ran beef cattle on this range for years.

The Woolley family took an active part in their rural community life, and George even served as a county commissioner. Many others moved into the area including some sheep ranchers. The cattlemen did whatever they could to discourage the sheep ranchers because sheep cropped grass right down to the roots and ruined grasslands for cattle.

Then George and Charles Woolley decided to try their hand at sheep raising.

An incident occurred in December 1911 that is typical of the range wars of this time. The young man left in charge of a group of sheep belonging to the Woolleys woke one morning to find that cattlemen had come during the night and bludgeoned and slashed to death all the sheep in the corral.

Even though the Woolleys had lived in Routt County for a long time and were respected citizens, their sheep were not spared. The five cattlemen who killed the sheep were never arrested. George and Charles Woolley left Craig soon after this sheep-killing incident and moved to Fort Morgan.

Queen Ann

Ann Bassett lived in a rugged area of extreme northwest Colorado known as Brown's Hole. This area stretches along the Green River and extends northwest to the borders of Wyoming and Utah. Here Ann Bassett's parents ran a small horse and cattle ranch. After her parents died, Bassett took over the ranch and soon earned the name of Queen Ann.

Queen Ann found herself in the middle of a range war. Large cattle companies tried to drive the smaller ranchers out. Bassett's fiancé, Matt Rush, whom some thought was a cattle rustler, was shot dead in his cabin. Many believed that Ora Haley, owner of the big Two Bar Ranch, had hired Tom Horn to kill Matt. Rumor had it that Horn received $500 per victim. Horn apparently also shot Isom Dart, a former slave who worked on the Bassett Ranch.

The famous outlaw Butch Cassidy and his gang came to hide out at Brown's Hole after his first major bank robbery. He was welcomed in the town and at the Bassett Ranch. Apparently Queen Ann, who was in a constant struggle to protect her cattle land, had no quarrel with bank robbers. Because she was openly kind and friendly to these outlaws, people became suspicious of her.

Ann Bassett was accused of being a cattle rustler. She was brought to trial and was acquitted. She continued to run the family ranch until her death in 1956.

Founding the Union Colony

Nathan C. Meeker was the agricultural editor for the *New York Tribune* newspaper. The editor-in-chief of the paper was Horace Greeley. Greeley is famous for a piece of advice he published in his paper in 1853: "Go west, young

man, go west." He was advising unemployed New Yorkers to go west and grow up with their country. It was Greeley who sent Nathan Meeker to Colorado to see if it might be a good place to start a farming community. Meeker liked what he saw.

On Meeker's return, the *New York Tribune* ran a front-page ad on December 14, 1869, asking people interested in farming in Colorado to come to a meeting. Eight hundred people attended. They decided to form the Union Colony, "limited to people of

Nathan Meeker. Courtesy of City of Greeley Museums, Permanent Collection

good character." Meeker was chosen president of the group. He and two others were sent ahead to pick out a site in Colorado for the colony.

After looking at several spots, they finally chose one in what is now Weld County. They picked a place near where the Poudre and Platte Rivers meet. And on March 15, 1870, they chose the name of Greeley for their town. The first settlers in Greeley arrived on April 18, 1870, and others soon followed. The streets were marked off with a plow, and people were allowed to choose a lot in town as well as a garden plot or piece of farmland. Until their homes were built, the Union colonists lived in tents.

In the Union Colony, everyone was to work together for the common good. They built houses, irrigation canals, tree-lined streets, and eventually a school, courthouse, and college. Many of these settlers became successful farmers. Today, Weld County has the richest farming and ranching land east of the Rockies. The people raise corn, beans, and have feedlots for cattle.

produce is grown on irrigated land. The plains in eastern Colorado offer big areas of fertile soil, but there is little rainfall. Farmers have found ways to bring water and irrigate some of this land. In other sections, farmers use special dry-farming methods.

Vegetables and Fruits

Colorado ranks fifth in the nation as the overall potato-producing state. Each year, Colorado grows 28 million pounds of potatoes. Colorado is also the nation's third largest carrot-producing state, and it ranks third in growing summer lettuce.

Today, Colorado ranks seventh in producing sugar beets. The peak of sugar-beet production in Colorado was in 1969. Sugar beets are still an important crop. The beets are used to make sugar, and the beet tops are used for livestock food. The tops are fed, along with grain and hay, to animals during the long winters. There used to be more than a dozen sugar factories in

Pulling sugar beets near Greeley.
Courtesy of Denver Public Library, Western History Collection, Llewellyn Moorehouse, Z-114

Colorado, with the largest belonging to the Great Western. Some of these factories are now closed.

In the nation, Colorado ranks sixth in the production of cantaloupes. It ranks seventh in growing pears, eighth in the production of tart cherries, and tenth in the growing of peaches.

Colorado's Grand Valley

Mesa County, which forms the western border of Colorado, is located where the Colorado and Gunnison Rivers meet. Its elevation is 4,588 feet. It is sometimes called the Grand Valley. At one time, this area was home to the Ute. But after Colorado became a state in 1876, more white people wanted to come and live on these lands, so the Native Americans were forced to move. They were ordered to be on reservations in northeast Utah and southwest Colorado by September 4, 1881.

After that date, many settlers poured in. One of the first was George A. Crawford. He and others mapped out a plan for the city of Grand Junction. Today, the three largest cities in the county are Grand Junction, Fruita, and Palisade.

Irrigation in the Grand Valley began in 1882. Canals were completed, bringing water from the Colorado River into the area. These canals turned this dry land into a rich farming region. Arthur E. Pabor is given credit as one of the first big fruit growers in the valley. In 1883, he planted apples, pears, peaches, cherries, plums, and grapes near Fruita. Many others followed, and the area is now known for its fruit production.

In the early days, the first markets for the various fruits were gold and silver mining camps. With the introduction of railroads, fruits were shipped throughout the country. By the early 1900s, thousands of boxcars of fruit were shipped by rail each year.

"Peach Days" celebrations were popular in the late 1800s and often featured a Peach Queen. One of the first big festivals held in the area occurred in 1895 when about 10,000 people came to hear the guest speaker, William Jennings Bryan. The festival continued to grow each year and, in 1909, when Peach Day was celebrated in Grand Junction, President William Taft was the guest of the town.

The peach festivals have continued, and today people from all over the country come to the Grand Valley in August to celebrate the Palisade Peach Festival. A sign at the edge of town announces, "Welcome to Palisade, the Peach Capital of Colorado."

During the festival you can get peach milkshakes and peach pies, but you can also be more daring and try peach salsa and peach tacos. The celebration often includes baking contests, art shows, and parades.

While peaches and pears grow along the mesas, they also grow in the floodplains of the Colorado and Gunnison Rivers. Apples, cherries, apricots, and plums grow on the western slope of the

Rockies. Berries are grown near large cities in the fruit areas of Colorado. Rocky Ford cantaloupes are another famous Colorado crop. And many greenhouses produce cut flowers and bulbs. These are especially important around large cities such as Denver.

Grains

In 2001, corn was the leading crop grown in Colorado in terms of total value. Hay was the second leading crop, and wheat ranked third. Colorado produces 9 million bushels of barley a year. Colorado ranks in the top ten states in the nation in growing

Grain storage elevators.

barley, sorghum grain, and silage, and all types of wheat. This helps make Colorado the number one beer-producing state in the country.

Molson Coors Brewing Company and Anheuser-Busch

The huge grain industry in Colorado gives rise to breweries. For example, the Molson Coors Brewery is an important and growing company in the state. Founded in 1873, the Adolph Coors Brewing Company merged with Molson, Canada's largest brewery, in 2004. Molson Coors products are available throughout the United States and in thirty international markets. Its

Coors brewery.

headquarters and main brewery, which is the largest single brewery in the world, is located in Golden, and the Molson Coors Brewing Company is a major employer in the metro Denver area.

Another brewery located in Colorado is Anheuser-Busch. The company, which started in St. Louis, has built several regional breweries. One of these, located in Fort Collins, Colorado, ships 6.1 million barrels annually.

Challenges Facing Colorado Farmers and Ranchers
In any given year, Colorado farmers face special problems with field crops. They may have to delay planting because of cold weather. Their crops may be caught in a killing freeze at the end of the season. Sometimes there are dry, late summers and falls, and this may lower the yield of crops.

Farmers in Colorado often rotate their crops. They might grow corn in a field, then during the next growing season they change and plant beans or sugar beets. Or they might raise alfalfa in a field and then switch to wheat. Rotating crops helps to keep insects and plant diseases under control.

Present-day ranching and farming remain major industries, but sometimes weather and other factors make the success of these endeavors as uncertain as prospecting for gold was in Colorado's early days.

Activities for Further Exploration

1. Many crops are important in Colorado. Different areas of the state hold festivals throughout the year to show off their crops to locals and to visitors. If you go on the Internet to http://www.ag. state.co.us/mkt/farmfresh/agfestivals.html you will find a current calendar of events that have been scheduled in the state such as Sugar Beet Days, Potato Days, and the large Palisade Peach Festival. You might be able to attend one of these agricultural events.

2. Farming methods have changed greatly over the years. Two interesting pictures showing these changes can be found at http://www.mii.org/pdfs/farming.pdf. If you have the chance to talk with someone who has been a farmer for many years, ask the farmer to tell you about the changes that have occurred.

3. Raising cattle and sheep was an important part of life in the early West. Colorado and many parts of the country experienced range wars. Two Coloradans often associated with range wars are Tom Horn and Queen Ann Bassett. To learn more, see http://www. wyomerc.com/bookranch/news/BR_Roundup_2.htm and http://www.fpcc.net/~sgrimm/ann_bassett.htm.

4. Brands were used to establish the ownership of cattle. Visit this Internet site to see some of these brands: http://www.barbwire museum.com/cattlebrandhistory.htm. Imagine that you owned your own cattle ranch. Choose a name that you might use for your own ranch and design your cattle brand.

Chapter 11
Colorado's Trees and Plants

Colorado has many different beautiful trees, as well as grasslands, lovely plants, and wildflowers. This variety is due in part to the

great differences in elevation throughout the state. There are long periods of cold and snow at the highest points, while low areas of the state are dry and desertlike. Different types of trees and flowers grow in each area.

The vegetation in Colorado grows in five basic life zones, although there are not sharp distinctions between these zones. Plants found in one zone gradually disappear as you move far enough either higher or lower in elevation. Western Colorado gets more rain than the eastern part of the state, and because of this, some flowers grow at lower elevations in the West than in the East.

Sunflower.

The Plains Zone
In the plains zone, where the soil is clay-like and sandy, the land is mostly flat and there is little rainfall. Few trees grow except for cottonwood, willows, and box elders along streams. Among plants found there are the

Prairie coneflower.

prairie coneflower, yucca, milkweed, sunflower, cactus, sand lily, prairie snowball, prickly poppy, and rabbitbrush.

133

Native American Use of Plants

The various plants, berries, and fruits of Colorado provided medicine and food for early Native Americans. Traditional healing herbs include many plant parts such as bark, roots, stems, flowers, fruits, seeds, and sap.

Early diaries indicate that *Ligusticum* root (lovage) was sometimes given as a gift and token of respect by Native Americans to early Spanish explorers in the Southwest and later to Colorado mountain men and trappers. The mountain men called *Ligusticum* root the "Colorado Cough Root." They chewed the root and also used it to make a tea that they drank as a cure for colds and flulike symptoms.

In the Spanish Peaks, Cherokee medicine women, known as *curandera*, used herbal remedies and passed on their knowledge to their children. Among that store of knowledge was the fact that Ocha is a root used to treat infection. Ruda is an herb that when blended with other herbs is used to make a liniment for aching muscles. *Manzanilla*, the Cherokee word for chamomile, is used to ease colic in babies.

Many tribes reveal their understanding of different plants and their properties through the stories that they tell. In a Cheyenne tale called "Fallen Star's Ears," a monster, wearing a necklace of human ears, is about to attack a Native village. To trick his enemy and win his trust, one of the tribe's warriors, Fallen Star, picks bracket fungus from trees and cuts them into the shape of ears, which he strings and wears as a necklace. Seeing the "ears," the monster trusts Fallen Star and then is caught in a trap.

According to the Cheyenne legend, ever since that time, the fungus that grows on trees is shaped just like ears. And it is true that the tree-ear fungus (*Auricularia auricula*) that grows in the moist forests of Colorado from dead trees on the forest floor is reddish and rubbery and resembles the skin of the human ear.

The Foothills or Transition Zone

Indian paintbrush.

Between the plains and the mountains is an area called the foothills, which is sometimes called the transition zone. The foothills receive more rain than the plains. Much of the soil here contains gravel and weathered rock. Yellow pine, scrub oak, and cottonwoods are common trees. Some of the many wildflowers are larkspur, grizzly bear cactus, yellow evening primrose, and Indian paintbrush.

The Montane Zone

Aspen in the snow.

The middle zone of the high mountains is the montane, where much of the soil is granite gravel. This montane zone gets twice as much rainfall as the plains. Great forests of lodgepole pine, spruce, and beautiful aspen grow here, and there are balsam and fir trees. It is in this area that the state flower, the columbine, grows best. Also growing here are the wood lily, mariposa, Indian paintbrush, yellow lady's slipper, fireweed, and shooting star.

Subalpine Zone

Guinn Mountain Trail conifers.

The subalpine life zone is between the montane zone and timberline. This area gets plenty of water. Because it is so high, snow stays late and frosts come early. The trees found here, Englemann spruce, limber pine, and alpine fir, are very small.

Colorado's Trees and Plants

135

Flowers in this area include the monkshead, glacier lily, fringed gentian, mountain marsh marigold, and little red elephants. This last-named plant has several dozen little pink or red flowerlets on a stalk. Each tiny blossom looks like the head of a pink elephant, complete with a long trunk.

Alpine Zone

The alpine life zone extends from timberline at about 11,500 feet to the highest peak at 14,431 feet. No full-sized trees grow at this high elevation. Lichens, mosses, and grasses live here, and flowers are usually tiny and close to the ground. Among the flowers found here are queen's crown, deer clover, alpine forget-me-not, sky pilot, and the arctic gentian.

Life Zones in Feet above Sea Level:
Alpine
Above 11,500 feet
Subalpine
10,500 to 11,500 feet
Montane
8,000 to 10,500 feet
Foothills
6,000 to 8,000 feet
Plains
3,500 to 6,000 feet

Colorado's Forests

Some ninety-eight kinds of native and naturalized trees grow in Colorado. Colorado's forests have many evergreens such as white fir, Douglas fir, balsam fir, Engelmann spruce, Douglas spruce, lodgepole pine, and ponderosa pine.

In the early history of Colorado, lumber was especially important. It was needed to build homes, for shoring up mine tunnels, and for making ties for the railroads that began to be built in many different parts of the state. Lumber is still important. Over the last

Rocky Mountain Columbine

The Rocky Mountain columbine (*Aquilegia caeruleas James*) is the state flower of Colorado. An early mention of this flower is found in the notes of Edwin James. He saw this lovely and delicate flower when he was a member of the first climbing party to go up Pikes Peak in 1820.

The blue-and-white Colorado Rocky Mountain columbine is a hardy perennial. Its flowers are one- to three-inches across, with backward-projecting spurs containing rich nectar, which makes the flower especially attractive to hummingbirds. The plant grows from one- to three-feet tall.

There are many species of columbine, and the flower grows in a broad range and a wide variety of colors. It is found on hot slopes and in shady forests.

On Arbor Day, April 17, 1891, Colorado schoolchildren voted for a state flower. Out of 22,316 votes that were cast, the Rocky Mountain columbine won with 14,472 votes. Second place went to a cactus. When a women's club in Cripple Creek realized that although the schoolchildren had chosen the columbine, it had not been officially designated as the state flower, they went to the legislature. Then it was formally adopted as the state flower on April 4, 1899.

The state song, "Where the Columbines Grow," was written by A. J. Flynn and adopted on May 8, 1915.

VERSE ONE

Where the snowy peaks gleam in the moonlight,
About the dark forests of pine,
And the wild foaming waters dash onward,
Toward lands where the tropic stars shine,
Where the scream of the bold mountain eagle
Responds to the notes of the dove
Is the purple robed West, the land that is best,
The pioneer land that we love.

CHORUS

'Tis the land where the columbines grow,
Overlooking the plains far below,
Where the cool summer breeze in the evergreen trees
Softly sings where the columbines grow.

The Creeping Trees

Have you ever heard of trees that creep? Many visitors cross the famous Trail Ridge Road in Colorado's Rocky Mountain Park without ever noticing one of its special wonders: the creeping trees. They may not move quickly, but this is one of several spots in the world where trees actually move.

These trees, which are mostly Englemann spruce, are called the krummholtz, or elfenwood, or are referred to as the dwarf forest. The word "krummholtz" is German for "twisted trees."

Krummholtz grow in the alpine zone in Colorado, which begins at about 11,500 feet. This area has long, cold winters and a short growing season. Winter cold combined with permafrost dwarfs the trees that grow at this elevation. And the harsh conditions create growth forms such as the krummholtz. Some trees grow so close to the ground that they resemble a mat.

Fierce winds kill branches on the windward side of these trees, giving them a flaglike appearance. Eventually, all the branches on one side of the tree are killed. And as the tree, or mat of trees, grows and reaches out horizontally on the non-windy side over a very long period of time, the trees actually creep away from the wind along their root systems.

The Bristlecones

Bristlecone pines are thought to be the oldest living things on our planet. They are found in Colorado, California, Utah, Nebraska, New Mexico, and Arizona.

In Colorado, bristlecone pines grow on Windy Ridge just west of Alma, in Pike National Forest. They can also be seen on Mount Evans, Berthoud Pass, James Peak, and Pikes Peak.

Ancient bristlecones are gnarled and twisted and live in very inhospitable areas where it is high and windy. They cling to the 11,700-foot ridge at the foot of Mount Bross, which rises up 14,000 feet.

The oldest of these trees, located in California, is close to 5,000 years old, which means that some bristlecone trees were taking root when the pyramids were being built. The oldest dated bristlecone in Colorado is estimated to be 2,436 years old. These trees are dated by dendrochronologists (tree-ring specialists) who count microscopic tree rings.

In Colorado, the Windy Ridge Bristlecone Pine Scenic Area was established in 1964 by the forest service. The bristlecones here rarely top forty feet and are thought to be between 800 and 1,000 years old. They often shed their bark and put out only a small spray of green. To the untrained eye, they may look dead.

fifty years, the amount of timber standing in U.S. forestlands has increased in the Rocky Mountain region.

The beautiful quaking aspen with its pale gray bark is found from the higher slopes to timberline. These aspen leaves turn a gorgeous golden color in the autumn. Crowds of people, both residents and visitors called "leaf peepers," go into the mountains in autumn to see these golden trees.

Along the rivers at lower elevations, many cottonwoods grow. In drier southern Colorado there are mountain cedars and piñon pine. Mountain ash and box elder thrive near the foothills. The blue spruce likes plenty of water, and it often grows along streams in the mountains.

About one-fifth of the state of Colorado is made up of national forests. Eleven national forests exist within the state and another national forest is shared with Utah. These forests cover 13,880,809 acres of land.

Forests continue to help Colorado meet its needs for lumber. They also provide habitat for birds, mammals, reptiles, amphibians, and fish. For many people, the most exciting thing about Colorado forests is that they are available for outdoor recreation, offering campgrounds, picnic areas, trails, and other facilities. Within the national forest system are wilderness areas that people can enjoy but which are closed to timber cutting and the use of any kind of vehicles. Colorado also has thirty-four national wilderness areas.

Colorado forests are also important to the state water supply. Having forests on the slopes of mountains causes the snow to melt slowly. Then the water can be stored in lakes and reservoirs as it melts and runs off to help provide a year-round water supply. After devastating fires wipe out forests, flooding often occurs.

Colorado also has two national grasslands. The headquarters for the Comanche Grasslands is in Pueblo, and the headquarters for the Pawnee Grasslands is in Fort Collins. Forest rangers manage these areas.

Colorado's many forests and grasslands, as well as its abundance of wildflowers, add to the spectacular beauty of the state.

Activities for Further Exploration

1. Colorado has many beautiful wildflowers. Many reference books have excellent color photographs or drawings. From an area where it is permitted, pick two of your favorite wildflowers. Using a reference book to help you identify them, draw colorful pictures of them. Among many available useful books are *Guide to Colorado Wildflowers, Vol. 1: Plains and Foothills* and *Guide to Colorado Wildflowers, Vol. 2: The Mountains*, both by G. K. Guennel.

2. In many stores, you can buy packets of wildflower seeds. Buy some seeds and potting soil, plant your seeds in plastic cups, and place them in a sunny kitchen window. Care for them, taking those that thrive and transplanting them in some appropriate area outdoors. An interesting resource is *Wildflowers of Colorado* by John Fielder.

3. On your next hike, look closely for wildflowers. Do not pick the flowers, but observe them carefully, take notes, and sketch some of them. If a camera is available, take photographs of the flowers. Notice the leaves and stems as well as the blossoms. A useful book to help you identify the different flowers that you find is *Wildflowers of North America: A Guide to Field Identification* by Frank D. Venning.

4. You can learn to identify evergreens by looking closely at their needles and cones. A good resource book is *Trees and Shrubs of Colorado* by Jack L. Carter. If you visit a national park or forest, a ranger may help you with your identification. You'll learn to look at the height and shape of the tree as well as its bark and needles.

Chapter 12
Colorado's Rivers

Many important rivers begin in Colorado. In fact, Colorado is sometimes called the "Mother of Famous Rivers." The first people to trap, trade, and explore Colorado followed its rivers like highways in the wilderness. Below you will read about a few of the seventy-eight large and small rivers found in the state of Colorado.

The Colorado River

The Colorado River is the major river of the American Southwest. It drains about 242,000 square miles of land in seven states. The Colorado River starts in the Grand Lake area of Colorado. It begins at an altitude of about 9,010 feet and flows southwest. The Green River is its primary tributary. Other tributaries are the Gunnison, Blue, Eagle, Roaring Fork, and Dolores.

The name *Colorado* means "colored red." The river was given that name by the Spanish. The Colorado River used to carry tons of silt, which gave it a reddish color. Much of that silt is now trapped by Glen Canyon Dam, which was built in 1963.

The Colorado River begins in the Rocky Mountains and travels 1,400 miles to the Gulf of California. On its way, it enters the Grand Canyon at Lee's Ferry. There the elevation of the river is 3,110 feet. This deep canyon was cut over millions of years. The river leaves at the other end of the Grand Canyon at Grand Wash Cliffs. The Colorado River has many rapids. But it also has calm stretches of water. Its depth varies from six to ninety feet. The average depth of the river is twenty feet.

The lower Colorado River was explored by Lieutenant Joseph C. Ives. The Colorado is often called the River of Mystery because it is so hard to travel up or down it.

The Arkansas River

The Arkansas River drains into southeastern Colorado. It begins above Leadville. By the time it reaches Granite, the Arkansas is a

John Wesley Powell

Who would have thought that a baby boy born in Mount Morris, New York, in 1834 with a Methodist minister for a father would grow up to be a war hero? And who would have thought that a Civil War veteran who had lost his arm would go on to be remembered as a mountain climber, champion of Native Americans, and explorer of the Colorado River? John Wesley Powell did all these things.

John Wesley Powell.
Courtesy of U.S. Geological Survey

As a child, Powell learned from his father to take a stand against slavery, and he learned to love and study nature. When he was twelve, his family moved to a farm in Wisconsin. Powell began teaching in a one-room school when he was eighteen. He saved money for college, taught at Hennepin, Illinois, in 1858, and in 1860 became super-intendent of schools. His quiet life changed when the Civil War began.

Powell was one of the first to volunteer and joined the 20th Illinois Infantry. He was soon made an officer. During the Battle of Shiloh, on April 5, 1862, he was wounded and his right arm had to be amputated below the elbow.

After the war, Powell became a professor of geology at Illinois Wesleyan University, lectured at Illinois State University, and became curator of the state natural history museum. In 1867, Powell led a group of students to the

Rocky Mountains to collect specimens for the museum. He also climbed Pikes Peak and camped for several weeks in South Park. Before returning to his academic life, Powell explored the headwaters of the upper part of the Colorado River.

In 1868, Powell returned to Colorado to collect more specimens and to climb Longs Peak. In October, he built a winter cabin on the White River about 120 miles above its mouth. While in this area, he made friends with the Ute. He compiled a dictionary of Ute vocabulary and learned to speak their language. The Ute gave him the name of Kapurats, or "One-Arm-Off." Years later he helped establish the Bureau of Ethnology, which sponsored important anthropological research regarding Native Americans.

Powell decided to explore the Colorado River by descending it in small boats. He had four boats built to his own design and selected a crew of nine. He began his journey on May 24, 1869, at Green River Station, Wyoming Territory. Powell's group traveled more than 1,000 miles of river through canyons and over rapids. They finished their trip on August 30 at the mouth of the Virgin River in Arizona.

Immediately Powell made plans for a second trip, which he made in 1871 and 1872. This time he took a surveyor and photographer with him and emerged with specimens, notes, and photographs. Powell published several books including *The Canyons of the Colorado*. He helped found the National Geographic Society and served as director of the U.S. Geological Survey from 1891 until 1894. Powell died in 1902 and is buried in Arlington Cemetery.

major river. It carves its way around boulders and through the mountains. As it flows south through the Arkansas River Valley, it passes six of Colorado's highest mountain peaks. It goes past Buena Vista and Salida. Then it turns east and flows through the Royal Gorge with its sheer rock walls where it is spanned by the world's highest suspension bridge.

After passing Cañon City, at Pueblo, the Arkansas River enters the plains. Eventually it wanders south to Kansas and Oklahoma, crosses Arkansas, and joins the great Mississippi River. Its important tributaries, which begin in the mountains southwest of Pueblo, are the St. Charles, Huerfano, Purgatoire, and Apishapa Rivers.

The Arkansas's 148-mile stretch in central Colorado is popular with those who like the outdoors. It is used for kayaking and rafting. It is also known as a great place to fish for brown and rainbow trout.

The Dolores River

The Dolores River flows for more than 200 miles through south-west Colorado. It begins high on Lizard Head Pass in the San Juan Mountains at 10,222 feet. The Dolores joins the Colorado River above Moab near the Colorado and Utah border. Part of the river has a great desert backdrop.

The Dolores runs north to McPhee Reservoir and then turns northwest. It flows through canyons of red sandstone cliffs. The Dolores is a popular river for outdoor activities such as canoeing and trout fishing.

The Eagle River

The Eagle River is a tributary of the Colorado River. The Eagle River begins on Tennessee Pass. It flows through Eagle Valley and the Beaver Creek Ski Area. Between Edwards and Dotsero, it flows through colorful sandstone cliffs. When the Eagle River meets the Colorado River, it makes the Colorado twice as big.

The Eagle River is used for outdoor recreation. People kayak, canoe, and raft on it. They also fish for rainbow, brown, brook, and cutthroat trout.

Colorado River Names

Many of Colorado's rivers have interesting names. The Frenchman River is sometimes called the Phantom River because it disappears and flows underground except when the area receives several inches of rain. It begins as Frenchman Creek near Holyoke.

The Cache la Poudre River was named by the French and means "hiding place of powder." Once, when caught in a winter storm, some French explorers left a supply of gunpowder there.

Big South Fork of the Cache la Poudre River.

The Chuchara River gets its name from the Spanish. It means "spoon." The Apishapa River was named by the Apache. It means "stinking water" and it is true that the water does smell.

The Purgatoire River can be seen near Trinidad. *Purgatoire* is a French word. There are many stories about how this river got its name from either the Spanish, the Mexicans, or from the French. It may be named because roiling water makes the red rocks of the area look like a fiery furnace. Or it may have been named for souls sent to purgatory.

Legend tells of a band of men, led by Captain Bonilla and Juan de Humana, who came to the Purgatoire River area in the service of Spain in 1596. One or more of the men was murdered under strange circumstances. Whether one man was killed by a member of his own party or whether he and others were killed by hostile Native Americans is uncertain. However it happened, the men died without receiving the last rites of the church. Legend has it that the souls of the murdered men still haunt the area, filling it with strange wailing sounds.

Since the name Purgatoire was hard to pronounce, some cowboys called it the Picketwire River, and some people still use that name for the river.

The Animas River may have been so named by Native Americans. The story of the Escalante Expedition refers to it as the Rio de las Animas, or the River of Souls. Their Indian guides told them that they called this "the river of the departed ones" because of the many ancient pueblos and cliff dwellings in the area.

The Mancos River was named for an early Spanish explorer who fell near the river and hurt his hand. *Mancos* is Spanish for "crippled" or "one-handed." *Yampa* is a Ute Indian word. Yampa is a plant like a wild onion that grows along the banks of the river. The Conejos River is a tributary of the Rio Grande. It starts at Lake Ann. *Conejos* is Spanish for "rabbit."

The Huerfano River begins near Gardner. It is named for Huerfano Butte. This volcanic rock is a landmark in the area. It stands up high and alone near the river. In Spanish, *huerfano* means "orphan."

The Big Thompson and Little Thompson Rivers are named after the Thompson brothers, one of whom was a big man while the other was a small man. Both brothers were killed by Ute Indians.

The Big Thompson Canyon Flood of 1976

The Big Thompson Canyon is a popular area west of Denver, Colorado. It is a twenty-five-mile canyon between Estes Park and Loveland. In 1976, on July 31, Coloradans were celebrating 100 years of statehood over a long week-end. It is estimated that several thousand people were hiking, fishing, camping, and driving through the Big Thompson Canyon on that day.

A thunderstorm accompanied by heavy rains hit the area. Weak upper winds did not push the thunderstorms eastward as they usually do, so rain continued to fall. Eight inches of rain fell in one hour.

The sheer rock slope of the canyon at a spot called the Narrows lacked soil and vegetation. Rain plummeted straight down the walls of rock into the canyon, and the river rose over its banks. The water was so strong it hurtled boulders that were ten feet across downstream. The flood came with almost no warning, and people who stayed in their cars were killed as vehicles were smashed and ripped to pieces.

At the Narrows, cars, parts of buildings, and other debris smashed into the supports of a 228,000-pound water pipe where it crossed above the river and highway. The roaring floodwaters carried the pipe a quarter of a mile downstream.

Within two hours, the flood had claimed the lives of 139 people with another six missing. Four hundred and eighteen houses were swept away and another 138 were damaged. Fifty-two businesses were wiped out. In all, there was $35.5 million in property damage.

Such a flood is considered a 10,000-year flood, which means that such an event is expected to happen only once every 10,000 years.

The Gunnison River

The Gunnison River is one of the main tributaries of the Colorado River. It begins in Almont where the East and Taylor Rivers meet. It flows through the Gunnison Valley and drains into Blue Mesa Reservoir. The Black Canyon of the Gunnison is one of America's newest national parks. At a point called the Narrows in this canyon, the river is only forty feet wide at river level. The walls of the canyon rise 1,700 feet up to the plateau. The Gunnison River was named for John W. Gunnison, a railroad surveyor.

The Gunnison joins the Colorado at Grand Junction. Its tributaries are the East River, Taylor River, Lake Fork, Cimarron River, North Fork, and the Uncompahgre River.

The North and South Platte Rivers

The North Platte River begins in North Park. It flows north into Wyoming. Then it turns east and southeast and joins the South Platte. The South Platte River starts near Alma and flows through northeastern Colorado. Important tributaries of the South Platte are Clear Creek, St. Vrain, Big Thompson, and Cache la Poudre. In North Platte, Nebraska, the North and South Platte Rivers join and flow into the Missouri River.

South Platte River.

The Rio Grande River

The Rio Grande River begins in the San Juan Mountains near Silverton. It flows 1,900 miles from there to the Gulf of Mexico. It is the third longest river in the United States and the fifth longest in North America.

Creede, a mining town, is the first city along the Rio Grande. The south fork begins on the east side of Wolf Creek Pass and joins the Rio Grande near the town of South Fork. The San Luis Valley of Colorado is an arid area. It gets its water from the Rio Grande and its tributaries through canals and ditches that cross the valley floor.

The Rio Grande River forms the boundary between Texas and Mexico. After leaving the San Luis Valley of Colorado, the Rio Grande flows through New Mexico. Then it flows along the southwestern Texas border all the way to the Gulf of Mexico.

The San Juan River

The San Juan River and its seven tributaries drain the San Juan Mountains in southwest Colorado. The San Juan starts near Wolf Creek Pass. Between Pagosa Springs and Pagosa Junction, it is joined by the Navajo and Rio Blanco Rivers. The Navajo Reservoir stores water to be used by farmers in the San Juan Basin, and after leaving the dam, the San Juan flows across northern New Mexico. At Farmington, it is joined by the Animas and La Plata Rivers.

The Yampa and White Rivers

The Yampa and White Rivers are a part of the Colorado River drainage area. They drain the far northern part of Colorado. The Yampa River, which begins in the Flattop Mountains, has several tributaries. They are the Elk, Elkhead, Little Snake, and Williams Fork Rivers.

The White River starts at Trappers Lake in the Flattop Wilderness Area. A tributary of the White River is Piceance Creek.

Colorado's many rivers continue to provide water for drinking and farming as well as allow people to raft, canoe, and fish in them.

Hot Springs

There are many hot springs in Colorado. Several Colorado towns have "Springs" in part of their names. Native Americans went to some of these springs for healing. Today, many of these springs are resorts where people come to enjoy the water.

Activities for Further Exploration

1. Although you may get to visit some sparkling streams and lovely waterfalls, don't drink the water because it is not safe. The drinking water in your home and school has to be treated to make it safe for drinking. Go to http://www.epa.gov/safewater/kids/index.html for an Internet site that explains more about water treatment.

2. John Wesley Powell was a famous explorer. His explorations on the Colorado River and through the Grand Canyon are especially interesting. See http://www.powellmuseum.org/MajorPowell.html for more information. A book of interest is *A River Running West: The Life of John Wesley Powell* by Donald Worster, Oxford University Press.

3. A filter is used to remove suspended substances from water. If you're interested, you can carry out a simple science experiment to show how this works. You will need two glasses, two coffee filters, water, a measuring cup, a teaspoon, a small amount of sand and sugar. Add 1 teaspoon of sand to a cup of water. Stir. Pour the sand mixture through the filter and into the glass. Note that the sand is trapped in the filter. Add a teaspoon of sugar to another cup of water. Stir. Pour the sugar mixture through the filter and into a second glass. Taste the water. Is the water sweet? Did the filter remove the sugar?

4. Floods are a danger in many parts of the United States. In Colorado, the Big Thompson flood is very famous. You can learn more about it at http://www.coloradoan.com/news/thompson, where you can view a media presentation.

Chapter 13
Colorado's Wildlife

Because of great differences in elevation, vegetation, and rainfall on the mountains, valleys, plains, and parks of Colorado, the state has many different kinds of animals and birds. Coloradans as well as visitors to this colorful state can find wildlife everywhere.

Fish
Many fish live in Colorado's lakes and reservoirs. There are bass, bluegill, carp, crappie, perch, and pike. White salmon and channel cats are found in the Yampa and Green Rivers.

Cold-water fish include the mountain whitefish and trout. There are rainbow, cutthroat, German brown, and brook trout. The rainbow trout makes up about three-fourths of the trout population.

The native trout is the cutthroat. It is a beautiful fish with bright markings and a reddish orange stripe at the throat. Cutthroat, although descriptive, is a strange and violent-sounding name. Because of its name, some people did not want the native cutthroat to become the state fish. They wanted the rainbow trout instead. But after many years, the cutthroat trout was selected to be the official state fish of Colorado.

Colorado's largest trout is the lake trout or Mackinaw. Another large fish is the kokanee salmon, which was introduced into the Granby, Green Mountain, and Skagway Reservoirs in 1951.

Birds
Pheasants live on Colorado's farmlands. Bobwhite quail are found in eastern Colorado along river bottoms. Scaled quail live on the plains and foothills of southwestern Colorado, and Gambel's quail are found in west-central Colorado.

Wild turkeys gobble in the pine forests and oak brush areas of southern and central Colorado. The white-tailed

Ptarmigan, winter.

153

The Dance of the Sage Grouse and Prairie Chicken

The sage grouse is a striking-looking bird. About the size of a small turkey, it has a black belly, long pointy tail feathers, and a ruffled white breast. The sage grouse is common in North Park in the north-central part of Colorado. People come great distances to observe the sage grouse "dance." One of the best places to see this is the Coalmont Sage Grouse Viewing Area.

In March and April, the sage grouse strut their stuff. They choose a low, open clearing that is surrounded by sagebrush. This spot, used for display or dancing, is called a lek. When it is lekking, the male sage grouse puffs itself up and reveals two yellowish neck sacs. Quickly it inflates and deflates these to cause a distinctive bubbly popping noise. Some people think that the noise sounds like someone gulping underwater.

As many as fifty sage grouse may participate in lekking just before daybreak. The dominant male in the group stands in the center of the lek. All the males raise their tail feathers in spiky fans, ruffle their wings, strut, and bob. Their chests puff up and the popping noise begins. Hens, attracted by the display, descend to breed.

The greater and lesser prairie chickens are smaller than the sage grouse but have a similar mating ritual. The neck sacs of the greater prairie chicken are golden in color while the lesser prairie chickens have reddish sacs. Males inflate and then deflate these sacs creating a deep booming sound that can be heard a great distance. At the same time, the prairie chickens perform intricate dancelike movements. They take a few tiny steps and then rapidly stamp their feet.

Greater prairie chickens are often observed in the northeastern prairie grasslands, while the lesser prairie chickens are common in the Comanche National Grasslands in the southeastern part of Colorado.

ptarmigan lives near and above timberline, and the chukar partridge lives on the western slope.

Three kinds of grouse live in Colorado. The sage grouse lives in sagebrush areas. The blue grouse is found in the forests of the Rocky Mountains, and sharp-tailed grouse live on both the eastern and the western plains.

Canada geese.

Important game birds include doves in the foothills and plains, ducks along the Platte and Arkansas Rivers, and geese in southeastern Colorado. Among the waterfowl that live in the state are the mallard, pintail, blue-winged teal, green-winged teal, and cinnamon teal. Other waterfowl found in the state include the gadwall, widgeon, wood duck, canvasback, Canada goose, and the whistling swan.

Also found in Colorado are eagles, hawks, falcons, and several kinds of owls. There are screech, burrowing, long-eared, and great-horned owls. Some birds come to Colorado in the spring and then leave again. Two of these are the band-tailed pigeon and the mourning dove.

Songbirds found in Colorado include the starling, western tanager, downy and hairy woodpeckers, and the horned lark. Other common songbirds are the mountain chickadee, American goldfinch, bluebird, robin, jay, meadowlark, song sparrow, and mockingbird.

Big Game Animals of Colorado

Colorado's early settlers ate the meat of buffalo, deer, elk, and antelope. More than 100 years ago, there were lots of game animals. Gradually, many of these were killed. Early in the 1900s, the state began to control hunting. Now many of the herds of wild animals, which were becoming very scarce, are increasing again.

One group of Colorado animals is called big game animals.

Among these are mule deer, which are common in Colorado. They are named for their large mulish-looking ears. The bucks shed their antlers in January and February. Does have twins in May or June. Mule deer eat sagebrush, bitterbrush, and mountain mahogany. Between their summer and winter homes, they may range 100 miles. They are hunted in the fall. Mule deer are the most abundant big game animal in the state.

Elk were called *wapiti* by the Native Americans. These animals are larger than deer. Both the bulls and cows have manes. They vary in weight from 400 to as much as 1,000 pounds. The back of an elk is yellow-brown. The legs, neck, and head are dark brown. These animals eat shrubs such as serviceberry and mountain mahogany, as well as grass. A single spotted calf is born to the cow in June.

A few white-tailed deer are found in grassy river bottoms. They are also found in the mountains on both sides of the

Elk, Rocky Mountain National Park.

Continental Divide and along the foothills of eastern Colorado. The tails of these animals are white underneath. White-tailed deer eat twigs, acorns, grasses, and weeds.

Moose are not native to Colorado but were brought into the state from Wyoming. They have scoop-shovel horns and bells of skin hang down from their throats. Some of these animals are found southeast of Walden, Colorado. They eat the bark of willows and birch and often dip down their great heads to munch on water plants.

Rocky Mountain goats came into Colorado from Montana, South Dakota, and Idaho. They have long hair with a woolly under-fur. These animals move slowly, but they can climb very steep cliffs. They do not shed their horns. Rocky Mountain goats are found in the Collegiate Peaks and in the Mount Evans area.

Pronghorn antelope live on the eastern plains and the north-

The Death of Samson, the Famous Elk of Estes Park

Samson the elk was a regular visitor to the Estes Park YMCA Center. Every year for six years the big elk summered in Grand Lake and spent the other eight months of

Samson the elk statue, Estes Park.

the year in Estes Park. At age twelve, Samson had an enormous set of eight-by-nine-point antlers. (This means that his antlers bore eight points on one side and nine points on the other side, which is exceptional.) At about 1,000 pounds, Samson was thought to be the largest bull elk in the valley.

Thousands of people had seen Samson and photographed him. He was used to humans, and residents and visitors to the Estes Park YMCA Camp almost thought of him as a pet. But in November 1995, a poacher shot and killed Samson with an arrow from a crossbow. Apparently, his intent was to sell the head and antlers as a trophy for several thousand dollars. When word got out of Samson's death, hundreds of people phoned the legal authorities demanding punishment.

The poacher was caught and tried. He was given ninety days in jail and six years of supervised probation. He had to pay $8,220 in fines and assessments and had to serve 360 hours of useful public service. The poacher lost his driving privileges for two years and his hunting privileges for six years. He was banned from owning any weapons, and his crossbow was taken and destroyed.

People from all over the country contributed to a fund to pay an Estes Park artist to make a memorial sculpture. The larger-than-life bronze sculpture of Samson was put in place at the east entrance to Estes Park and was officially dedicated in September 1997.

west plateau. There are only 11,000 to 15,000 of these animals left. Both does and bucks have horns. Antelope are light colored and not spotted. They are very fast runners, reaching speeds of fifty miles an hour. Pronghorn antelope eat weeds, herbs, and cactus fruit.

Colorado has the largest herd of bighorn sheep in North America. These animals climb well on high cliffs. People sometimes spot bighorns in Rocky Mountain National Park. They also live in the Glenwood Springs area, in the Sangre de Cristo Mountains, and in Poudre Canyon, where they eat grasses, weeds, and shrubs.

Bighorn rams weigh between 200 and 300 pounds. Bighorn sheep keep their horns instead of shedding them, and the horns keep growing. Rings on the horns show the age of the sheep. Lambs are born in May and June, and when they are only three days old, they are able to climb easily on cliffs.

Fur-Bearing Animals

Many of the animals in Colorado were valued for their fur. Beavers were trapped in great numbers for their pelts. A beaver weighs between thirty and forty pounds. Beavers eat aspen, cottonwood, and willow branches, aquatic plants, grasses, and roots. They have big, flat tails and are famous for building dams and lodges. Young beavers live with their parents for two years.

Muskrats live in streams and marshes where they build mounds made of cattails. Then they make nests inside the mounds. Each year, the muskrat may have two or three litters of babies.

Minks also live in or near the water where they catch frogs, crayfish, muskrats, fish, mice, and rabbits. They make their homes in stream banks. Four to five babies are born at one time. Many minks are now raised on fur farms, and their pelts are used for fur coats.

Martens live in the high country and are seldom seen below 9,000 feet. They live in spruce forests and hunt mostly at night. They spend much of their time in trees and often make a den high above the ground in a hollow tree. Martens eat mice, shrews, rabbits, insects, birds, and berries. In the spring, their young, called "kittens," are born.

Masters of Camouflage

One way various birds and animals keep safe is to blend in with their surroundings so that they cannot be seen by predators. Some of the wildlife of Colorado are masters of camouflage. They change their fur or feathers to blend in with the surroundings in changing seasons.

Ptarmigan.

Weasels live from the eastern plains of Colorado to the mountains. There are both long-tailed and short-tailed weasels. The long-tailed weasel is about fourteen to eighteen inches long and weighs about seven ounces, while the short-tailed weasel is only eight to ten inches long and weighs about three ounces.

Weasels have three to eight babies in the spring. They eat mice, shrews, chipmunks, ground squirrels, nesting baby rabbits, and baby birds that live in nests on the ground. A weasel wraps its long body around its prey and kills it with a quick bite at the base of the skull.

In summer, the coat of a weasel is red-brown, but then in winter it turns pure white except for the black tail tip. This white fur is called ermine. It is very hard to spot ermine in the snow.

The snowshoe hare is found only in North America. In Colorado, snowshoe hares live in subalpine forests. In summer they blend in with their surroundings with their grayish brown fur. During winter, their fur turns white. With white fur against white snow, they are very difficult to see.

These hares are up to two feet long and weigh six to nine pounds. For hares, they have relatively short ears but they have huge hind feet. They eat herbs, bark, and woody twigs and they produce two litters of five young each year. Snowshoe hares are food for coyotes, bobcats, foxes, and large hawks and owls.

Ptarmigan.

White-tailed ptarmigan live in the alpine areas of Colorado above treeline in summer when they eat leaves and seeds of various plants. In winter, they move to lower elevations and eat the buds, leaves, and twigs of willows.

White-tailed ptarmigan are stocky, chickenlike birds that are about ten inches in length. They are a mottled brown-gray color and blend in well against rocks most of the year. In winter, their feathers turn white and their legs and toes are heavily feathered, which makes it look as if they are wearing snowshoes.

The black-footed ferret is another member of the weasel family. It grows to be about twenty inches long. Ferrets are tan with black mask markings over the eyes. The coats of these animals do not turn white in winter as the weasel's does. The ferret eats prairie dogs. Ferrets often live in an old prairie dog tunnel or find some other underground den.

Other Mammals

Skunks are also members of the weasel family. The smell of this animal has made it famous. The hog-nosed skunk, the common striped skunk, and the spotted skunk live in Colorado. Skunks travel mostly at night. They eat insects and mice.

The black bear of Colorado is not always black. Sometimes these bears are cinnamon or brown. Usually they are found at about 5,000 feet. They grow to weigh between 250 and 450 pounds, but when they are first born during their mother's winter nap, little black bears weigh only about ten ounces. By spring, the two or three cubs are ready to travel with their mother. They move fast and can climb trees. They eat grasses, berries, honey, insects, and decaying meat.

Bears sometimes cause problems for residents. They are common in areas that have a lot of open space. Sometimes wildlife workers need to remove or kill bears that get used to being around humans and their food and become a nuisance or threat.

There may be a very few grizzly bears in the San Juan Mountains. These bears have a hump and mane over their shoulders. They are yellowish to black in color with silver-tipped hairs. Grizzly bears have especially long front claws and are very dangerous.

Cottontails and jackrabbits are found in Colorado. Because they eat plants and sometimes damage fruit trees, rabbits often are a problem to farmers. They are hunted, and about 250,000 cottontails are killed every year. Four to six young are born in a litter. A mother rabbit may have two to four litters of young in a year. The young of the rabbits are often caught and eaten by hawks, owls, coyotes, skunks, and weasels.

The badger is an animal with strange markings on its face. Badgers are known to be great fighters. They are fine diggers and have strong front legs and heavy claws. They dig out and eat ground squirrels, prairie dogs, and kangaroo rats. In May or June, two or three young are born. At one time, a badger pelt was worth $25. Shaving brushes were once made from badger bristles, but few people use these brushes today.

The opossum lives along river bottoms. The brand-new baby of an opossum is only about as big as a bee. The mother opossum carries her young around in a pouch. This animal is a marsupial, and all marsupials have pouches for their young. Opossums make nests of leaves in logs or trees. One of the funny things that they do is play dead to fool their enemies. Opossums will eat anything, including meat, fruit, and vegetables.

Raccoons are known by the bandit masks on their faces. They hunt at night and eat crayfish, frogs, insects, mice, and wild fruit. They make their dens among the rocks, in holes, or in hollow trees. Raccoons are good swimmers and good climbers. There are many raccoons on the eastern slope of Colorado.

Ring-tailed cats are found in rocky canyons where water is available on both the eastern and western slopes. These animals have a head like a fox and a body like a squirrel. The tail is ringed, and it is so big that it can curl all around the animal when it sleeps. Some people keep ring-tailed cats as pets. They catch mice and eat small mammals, birds, and fruit. Their homes are dens in hollow trees.

The bobcat lives along river bottoms and in the lower mountains of Colorado. Bobcats usually weigh fifteen to twenty-five pounds. Sometimes they reach forty pounds. They have little tufts of hair in their ears. Bobcats travel at night. They eat rabbits, rats, mice, and sometimes lambs, calves, and deer.

The Colorado Division of Wildlife is reintroducing the lynx to Colorado. They are moving a few lynx from Alaska and Canada to the southwest corner of Colorado. Trapped in winter, these lynx are released in the spring in the San Juan Mountains.

The mountain lion has many names. Some people call it a cougar, catamount, painter, puma, or panther. These lions eat deer. The mother has two spotted kittens. The kittens are born blind and can see when they are about ten days old. The kittens stay with their mother for the first two years.

Coyotes are found in the high mountains and on the plains. They eat meat, fruit, and plants. Their dens are made in caves and hollow logs. In April, five or six young, called pups, are born.

There are three kinds of foxes in Colorado. The kit fox is found in the semidesert area of southeastern Colorado. The gray fox lives along the edges of rivers and in the foothills, and the red fox lives in the high mountains. Foxes eat mice, rabbits, birds, fruit, and vegetables.

Coyote.

Marmot.

Other Colorado animals include porcupines, chipmunks, squirrels, prairie dogs, marmots, and pika. Some of these animals, such as prairie dogs, have lost much of their space as houses and shopping centers are built. There are wildlife specialists who are sometimes asked to move a whole prairie dog colony.

Snakes, Turtles, and Lizards

Most of the twenty-five species of snakes that live in Colorado are harmless. These include the striped whipsnake, several kinds of garter snakes, the lined snake, and the western hognose snake. There are also northern water snakes, corn snakes, racers, and the common kingsnake.

There are two poisonous snakes in Colorado. These are the western rattlesnake and the massasauga rattlesnake. The massasauga is found in southeastern Colorado. Western rattlesnakes are found throughout the state. The bite of a rattler can be fatal. Rattlesnakes are often found where there are large rocks and sunny spots. They live where there is a good rodent population to supply them with food. Bullsnakes are often mistaken for rattlesnakes.

There are many turtles in Colorado. These include the box turtle, painted turtle, snapping turtle, and yellow mud turtle. Lizards are common in dry areas. There are Texas horned lizards, desert spiny lizards, eastern fence lizards, and the Great Plains skink.

The diversity of Colorado in terms of climate and elevation provides an exciting array of birds and animals in all parts of the state.

Activities for Further Exploration

1. Look for birds on your hikes and in your yard. Find out which birds are common where you live. A bird identification book would be useful to have. So would a recording of common bird-calls. A helpful tool is *Birds of North America: A Guide to Field Identification, Revised and Updated*, Chandler S. Robbins.

2. Maybe you would want to build a bird feeder for your yard or for an appropriate place on the school grounds. A helpful book to consult for this project is *Birdhouses & Feeders You Can Make* by Paul Gerhards. You can also get directions to build a simple platform feeder with roof on the Internet at http://birding.about.com/library/weekly/aa011403a.htm.

3. Find out more about some of the creatures that live in Colorado. You might want to make drawings of your favorite ones and make your own book of Colorado creatures. A useful reference book is *Pocket Naturalist Colorado Wildlife: An Introduction to Familiar Species of Birds, Mammals, Reptiles, Amphibians, Fish and Insects* by James Kavanagh.

4. Listen to birdcalls and see if you can imitate them. Can you learn to identify a bird by its call? Many recordings are available and some of these can be checked out from libraries. One of many possible resources available is *53 All-American Bird Songs and Calls*, an audio CD from the Special Music Label.

Chapter 14
Colorado Statehood and State Symbols

During most of the 1700s, people thought that the land west of Missouri was worthless. Then in 1803 a very large piece of land known as the Louisiana Purchase was bought by the United States from France. A part of this land would later become the state of Colorado. But statehood did not come quickly or easily.

First, explorers came West. In 1806, Lieutenant Zebulon Pike was sent to look at lands that are part of what is now Colorado. In 1819, the border between the United States and the Spanish possessions was the Arkansas River, and Major Stephen Long was sent by the U.S. government in 1820 to explore this area.

Although more and more people began moving West, creating new states took time. Before statehood was possible, various claims to the land had to be considered. In 1821, Mexico became free of Spain, but it was not until 1848 that Mexico gave up her claims to parts of Colorado, and yet another piece of Colorado was obtained from the Republic of Texas after it became a state.

Many people thought of Colorado as the Pikes Peak Territory, but in fact the area that is now the state of Colorado was part of four different territories. The people in Denver and the middle-eastern section of this land were part of the Kansas Territory. Those in Boulder and in the northeastern part of the area were in the Nebraska Territory. The western slope of Colorado was in Utah Territory. The part south of the Arkansas River, which went across the San Luis Valley as well as across the eastern slope of the river, was in New Mexico Territory.

After the gold rush in 1859, there was considerable talk of the desirability of making Colorado a state. One of the first meetings to discuss this was held in Auraria on April 11, 1859. Over the next several years, there were many tries to at least get the U.S. government to make Colorado a separate territory, but they all failed.

People who lived in Colorado had no government offices close by, so as they needed them, they made their own rules. Mining was organized into mining districts. Miners made rules about how large a claim could be, and they had a recorder keep a record of who owned each claim. The farmers had their own claim clubs. They made rules to settle arguments over land and water rights.

Although this rather informal approach worked, many people still wanted Colorado to be organized into an official territory. Bills to accomplish this were presented in Congress in 1858 and 1859, but these bills did not pass and become law. At this time in our nation's history, arguments were going on about whether slavery would be allowed in the western lands, and this debate held up the formation of new territories.

Some people in Colorado got tired of waiting. They finally formed what they called the Jefferson Territory, and the residents elected Robert W. Steele as governor. But the U.S. Congress did not recognize this new territory, and since it was not official, many people wouldn't pay taxes or obey its laws.

In 1860, Kansas finally became a state, and the new western border of Kansas did not include the land that is now Colorado. It seemed as if the time was right at last to form a Colorado Territory.

Several names were proposed. Some wanted to call the new territory Tahosa, which means "people who live on the mountaintop." Others proposed naming it Arapaho for the Native American tribe. Still others thought it should be named after a famous person such as Jefferson. But when President James Buchanan signed a bill in 1861 creating a new territory, it was named Colorado.

Major William Gilpin became the first territorial governor of Colorado. He was named to this post by President Abraham Lincoln. Hiram P. Bennet was elected to represent the Colorado Territory in Washington, D.C. The first territorial legislature met in Denver on

Old Colorado City.

September 9, 1861, and they created the first seventeen counties of the state of Colorado.

The Territorial General Assembly decided to locate the capitol of the new territory at Colorado City, which was between Colorado Springs and Manitou Springs. The second legislative assembly met in Colorado City on July 7, 1862. These men came by foot, horseback, wagon, and stagecoach. They first met in a log cabin, and then they moved their meeting place to the Lucy Maggard Hotel.

On August 14, 1862, Golden City became the capital of the Colorado Territory. The legislature met there until 1867, when finally Denver was named as the capital. Between 1861 and 1876, Colorado had eight territorial governors. Offices were scattered about Denver, and the legislature met where it could find space.

Although Colorado became a territory just in time to enter the Civil War on the side of the Union, it did not take a very active part in the war. Governor Gilpin did organize some men into an army of volunteers, because it was feared that the Confederates might try to take Colorado.

Although many people were glad that Governor Gilpin had raised an army, he couldn't pay the soldiers. He had promised that the U.S. government would pay the men, and the government refused. Because of this, many people in Colorado wanted a new governor, so in 1862 President Lincoln appointed John Evans to be governor of Colorado.

The new governor had many important tasks to deal with, such as problems between Native American and settlers and making deals to connect Denver to other cities by railroads. Although it was evident that a new state capitol building was needed, his many pressing tasks kept the governor from spending much time thinking about this. That job was left to a future governor.

Land for the State Capitol

Deciding it was time to build a state capitol at last, Governor Hunt of Colorado appointed a three-man Capitol Commission in 1867 to secure land for the building. Mr. Harry C. Brown, a successful real estate man who later built the famous Brown Palace Hotel, donated ten acres at East Colfax and Lincoln Streets in Denver on January 11, 1868. Brown hoped having the capitol in this spot would increase the value of the adjacent land that he owned. But no funds were available, and so no capitol was built.

More people kept moving into the state. Jerome Chaffee, the Colorado Territory delegate to Congress, asked that Colorado be made a state. The U.S. Congress approved this request on March 3, 1875. People in Colorado then took part in a convention. They made rules for the new state. One question they discussed was whether women should be allowed to vote. They decided only men could vote. (This was changed in 1893 when Colorado became the second state to allow women to vote.) Colorado voters approved their new constitution on July 1, 1876.

President Ulysses S. Grant signed the law that made Colorado the thirty-eighth state of the United States on August 1, 1876. Since Colorado became a state 100 years after the United States became a nation, Colorado got the nickname of the "Centennial State."

The last territorial governor, John L. Routt, became the first governor of the state of Colorado. The state's first two senators were Jerome B. Chaffee and Henry M. Teller. A general election was held in 1881 to choose the capital city. In that vote, Denver won with 30,248 votes, while Pueblo, with 6,047 votes, was the second choice.

Years had passed since Brown had donated the land, and he was tired of waiting for a capitol to be built. He had originally said if $50,000 worth of improvements were not made to the land he'd donated, he'd revoke the deed. Since no construction had begun, Brown put a wooden fence around his ten acres and filed to reclaim his land. It took another seven years of trials and appeals before the

State capitol.

Supreme Court ruled against him. Plans were finally made to build the state capitol.

July 4, 1890, marked a huge celebration in Denver. There was a big parade and all the downtown buildings were draped in flags and buntings. Twenty mules pulled the twenty-ton cornerstone of the state capitol into place. Many items were placed in the cornerstone including a copy of the Colorado and U.S. Constitutions, a map of Colorado, gold coins, and newspapers.

After all the speeches were made, a big barbecue was held in Lincoln Park. Construction had begun!

After this, work on the capitol building went ahead quickly. By November 1894, the governor and others moved into their offices as work continued on other parts of the capitol. All the building materials came from Colorado except for the brass and oak trimmings. The granite came from Gunnison. The foundations and walls were made of Fort Collins sandstone, and Colorado onyx was used on the pillar facings.

The Capitol Dome—Green or Gold?

The capitol was finally considered finished when its dome was built. The dome was sheathed in copper, and when it tarnished, it turned to a dull green. In 1908 it was gilded with 200 ounces of pure gold. Eventually, this gold wore off and gold leaf was applied again in 1950 and in 1982.

Symbols

In addition to a state capitol building, Colorado, like other states, has many official state emblems and symbols. These are officially adopted by the members of the Colorado General Assembly or by order of the governor, although they are sometimes chosen after schoolchildren and their teachers propose a new symbol to the legislature.

The State Animal

In 1961, the Colorado General Assembly chose the bighorn sheep as the official animal of Colorado. The Rocky Mountain bighorn sheep is found only in the Rockies. It usually lives in the mountains above timberline. The male sheep, or ram, weighs up to 300 pounds while the female is a little smaller. Males stand about three and a half feet high at the shoulder.

Bighorn sheep displayed at the Denver Museum of Nature and Science.

The name "bighorn" comes from the fact that these sheep have large horns. The horns curve backward from the forehead and then turn down and curl forward. Sometimes an old ram may have horns that are fifty inches long.

The State Bird

The state bird of Colorado is the lark bunting. It was adopted as the official state bird on April 29, 1931. The male bird is black with a white patch on each wing, while the female is gray-brown and looks much like a song sparrow. In winter, the male bird changes color, becoming gray-brown like the female. But it still has some black markings on its chin and belly. The male bird is six to seven inches, and the female is a little smaller.

Lark buntings mostly live in the prairies of eastern and north-eastern Colorado, but they can be found at up to 8,000 feet in elevation. They make their nests on the ground. During courtship, the male warbles and trills a mating song. Lark buntings migrate south in the fall and return to Colorado in April or May.

The State Flag

The state flag was adopted on June 5, 1911. It is blue, white, red, and gold. There are three equal-width horizontal stripes. The middle one is white, and the outer two are blue. There is a circular red "C" on the flag. This "C" has a diameter that is two-thirds the width of the flag. A gold disk completely fills the inside of the "C." The flag was designed by Andrew Carlisle Johnson.

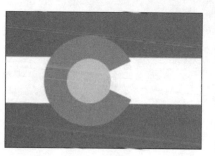

Colorado's state flag.

The white in the flag stands for the state's snowcapped mountains. The blue stands for clear, blue skies, and the red is for Colorado's reddish soil. The yellow stands for the sun. Attached to the flag is a cord of gold and one of silver. These cords are intertwined and have tassels.

The State Fish

From 1954 until 1994, the rainbow trout was considered the state fish, but on March 15, 1994, the general assembly made the greenback cutthroat trout the official state fish. The greenback cutthroat trout used to be common in creeks, streams, and rivers of the state. Many of these fish were caught. Mine tailings in the streams polluted the waters and killed some of the cutthroat. Other species of trout were brought into Colorado waters and helped to crowd them out. As a result, the cutthroat became almost extinct.

Then in the early 1990s, green cutthroat trout were found in a few streams in Rocky Mountain Park. These fish are now protected, and there are plans to introduce them to other waters within the state.

The State Flower

The white-and-lavender columbine is the state flower. It was officially adopted by an act of the general assembly on April 4, 1899. To protect the flower, the law prohibits digging or uprooting it on public lands. It is also unlawful to pick the columbine on private land without the consent of the landowner.

Some people buy seeds and plant wild columbine. Columbines in yards grow in many different colors. In the wild, columbines grow in blue, lavender, white, and even red, although red ones are not common. The state flower has outside petals that are a lavender blue while the inside petals are white with a yellow center.

Columbine.

The State Fossil

Stegosaurus is the Colorado state fossil. Scientists believe the stegosaurus weighed around ten tons. It was about as long as a bus and had a very small head. Stegosaurus ate plants and used a powerful beaked mouth. Its two back legs were longer than its two front legs. A row of large, pointed plates ran down its back, and there were also spikes on the tail, which it used for defense.

Stegosauruses lived in Colorado 150 million years ago. The Denver Museum of Nature and Science has a stegosaurus skeleton on display. The bones were found by a teacher and students from Cañon City High School.

The Kids Who Wouldn't Quit

In January 1980, a group of fourth graders at McElwain Elementary School in Colorado were studying about dinosaurs. They didn't forget about their favorite dinosaur when they became fifth graders the next year and studied the procedures of taking a bill through the legislature. And when they were sixth graders, they vigorously campaigned with T-shirts, bumper stickers, and exhibits to make stegosaurus the state fossil. They drew lots of support to their cause.

In front of "the kids who wouldn't quit," Governor Richard D. Lamm issued an executive order on April 28, 1982, establishing stegosaurus as the official Colorado state fossil.

The State Folk Dance

An act of the general assembly on March 16, 1992, made the square dance the official state folk dance of Colorado. The square dance is the most popular folk dance of the United States. It is traditionally accompanied by a fiddle, accordion, banjo, and guitar with instructions for a variety of movements given by a "caller."

The State Gemstone, Mineral, and Rock

The aquamarine is the official state gemstone. It was adopted on April 30, 1971, by an act of the general assembly. This gemstone can be found on the mountain peaks of Mount Antero and the White Mountains in Colorado. The granite rock in this area contains pegmatite bodies, which have cavities that contain crystals. The aquamarine crystals come in different colors. They range from light blue to pale green and deep green. Some crystals are very small while others may be six centimeters in length. On April 17, 2002, Colorado Governor Bill Owens signed a bill passed by the general assembly making rhodochrosite the state mineral. This mineral, found in some gold and silver ore–bearing veins, is deep red to pink in color. The largest rhodochrosite crystal in the world is on display at the Denver Museum of Nature and Science. In 2004, Girl Scout Troop 357 of Lakewood petitioned the legislature to make yule marble the official state rock. Employees of the Colorado Geological Survey presented testimony about the special characteristic of this marble. Some of the floor and trim in the state capitol building is made of yule marble, and it was also used in the Denver courthouse. This type of marble was also used in the Lincoln Memorial and the Tomb of the Unknowns. The bill passed and was signed by the governor. So Colorado has official red, white, and blue symbols with a red state mineral (rhodochrosite), a white rock (yule marble), and a blue gemstone (aquamarine).

The State Grass
Blue grama grass was adopted as the official state grass on May 20, 1987. It is native to the state of Colorado where it grows on both sides of the Continental Divide. Grasslands are an important resource of the state.

The State Insect
On April 17, 1996, the Colorado hairstreak butterfly was approved as the official state insect. This butterfly is found on both sides of the Continental Divide and lives between 6,500 and 7,500 feet. The butterfly is about two inches in width. It has purple wings with black borders and orange spots in the corner. There is blue on the underside.

The State Motto
The state motto, which appears on the state seal, is *Nil Sine Numine*. This Latin phrase is commonly translated as "Nothing without Providence." The motto is credited to the first territorial governor of Colorado, William Gilpin. It is drawn from Virgil's *Aeneid*, Book II.

State Nickname
Colorado's nickname is the Centennial State. It gets this name because Colorado became a state in 1876, 100 years after our nation's Declaration of Independence.

Colorado is a Spanish word that means "colored red." It was chosen for the name of the territory in 1861 by Congress.

Colorado is also called Colorful Colorado. This refers to the beauties of the state, including snowy mountains, golden prairies, green trees, and bright blue skies. The words "Colorful Colorado" appear on many signs, maps, and souvenirs.

The State Seal
The seal of the state of Colorado is a circle, and it is very much like the seal adopted by the First Territorial Assembly on November 6, 1861. The current state seal was adopted by the general assembly on

177

March 15, 1877. Only the Colorado secretary of state may affix this great seal to any document.

Colorado's state seal.

The seal is two and one-half inches in diameter. At the top is the eye of God within a triangle. Golden rays come down on both sides. Below the eye is a scroll. There is a symbol of the Roman fasces, which represents a republican form of government. There is a bundle of birch and elm rods, which stands for strength. There are also an axe, a shield, three snowcapped mountains and clouds, a miner's pick, and a sledgehammer. On a red band are the words "union and constitution." Also included are the state motto and the date when Colorado became a state, 1876.

The State Song

The words and music to the state song, "Where the Columbines Grow," were written by A. J. Flynn. It was adopted as the official state song on May 8, 1915 by an act of the general assembly.

Arthur J. Flynn, who wrote the words and music to the song, was born in New York and moved to Central City in 1889. The song was first publicly performed in 1916. There have been several attempts over the years to replace this song with another, but all these attempts have failed.

The State Tartan

An official state tartan was adopted by an act of the general assembly on March 3, 1997. A tartan is checkered or cross-barred woolen cloth worn to identify different clans of people in the Scottish Highlands. Colorado's colorful tartan pattern contains green, blue, black, lavender, white, gold, and red. The tartan is Celtic and may be worn by any resident or friend of the state of Colorado. July 1 is designated as Tartan Day.

The State Tree

The Colorado blue spruce was named as the state tree by Colorado schoolchildren on Arbor Day in 1892, but it was not officially made the state tree by an act of the general assembly until March 7, 1939. It was named by the botanist C. C. Parry.

Blue spruce.

The Colorado blue spruce is a silver-blue color and is sometimes called a silver spruce. It grows singly and in small groves and likes plenty of water. The blue spruce often grows along streams in the mountains. In the northern parts of its range it grows from 6,000 to 9,000 feet. In the southern parts of its range it is found at 8,000 to 11,000 feet.

Activities for Further Exploration

1. Colorado has a very distinctive state flag. If you go on the Internet to http://www.enchantedlearning.com/usa/states/colorado/outline you will find a flag that you can print out and color. To learn more about the history of this flag, visit http://www.50states.com/flag/coflag.htm.

2. The state gemstone is the aquamarine. You may wish to look in rock and gemstone books to try to find a book with a picture of this gemstone that shows aquamarine crystals and tells how they are formed. A useful resource is *Encyclopedia of Rocks, Minerals, and Gemstones* by Henry Russell.

3. John Routt was the last territorial governor and the first state governor of the state of Colorado. To learn more about him, visit the Internet at http://www.colorado.gov/dpa/doit/archives/govs/routt.html.

4. Much land was added to the United States of America through the Louisiana Purchase. Can you find out which current states in the United States were created from this land, which was purchased from France? A useful resource is *Louisiana Purchase* by Connie Roop, Peter Roop, and Sally Wern Comport.

Chapter 15
Contemporary Colorado

Colorado's current economy relies not only on its historic farms, ranches, and mines but also on tourism, manufacturing, and on var-

ied businesses, industries, and governmental offices. Many of these activities involve high technology. Well-educated employees are in demand. Instead of the old one-room school-house, students now receive their education through a wide range of colleges, universities, and

Denver skyline.

other institutes of learning. Contemporary Colorado continues to provide the setting for tales as exciting as those of its past.

Tourism

Tourism is a big industry in Colorado, and many visitors have become familiar with the Denver skyline as they fly into the state for pleasure and business. In 2000, visitors from within the United States spent $6.9 billion in Colorado. They spent their dollars on lodging, eating, drinking, transportation, recreation, and retail purchases. Tourists spent $1.3 billion on ski-related trips alone. The three states that send the most visitors to Colorado are California, Texas, and Illinois.

An additional $830 million was spent in the year 2000 by international visitors to the state. The largest number of international visitors to Colorado come from Mexico, Canada, the United Kingdom, Germany, and Japan. People come to the Mile High City to visit attractions such as the U.S. Mint, zoos, botanical gardens, and museums and to attend arts and sporting events.

John Elway, Super Bowl Superstar

There is no bigger name in the history of Colorado sports than that of John Elway, former quarterback for the Denver Broncos football team. Elway was born on June 28, 1960, in Port Angeles, Washington, and attended Stanford University where he was named an All-American football player. He soon joined the Denver Broncos where he was famous for last-minute game-winning scoring drives.

During the sixteen years he played for the Denver Broncos, Elway led his team to three Super Bowl losses and then back-to-back wins in Super Bowl XXXII and XXXIII. In Super Bowl XXXIII, John Elway was named Most Valuable Player. He holds numerous sports records including being one of only two quarterbacks to throw for more than 50,000 yards in his career. In 1992, Edge NFL named John Elway Man of the Year. Elway was elected to the Pro Football Hall of Fame in 2004.

Although he is retired from football, Elway owns an arena football team called the Colorado Crush. He also remains active in Colorado where he owns several automobile franchises and where he heads the Elway Foundation. This foundation raises $1 million annually to help Denver area women and children who are victims of abuse. He also is active with the Colorado School Coalition where he started the John Elway Drive for Education Scholarship Fund. The fund enables a number of high school graduates to attend college at Denver's Auraria Campus.

High Technology

A 2001 survey collected by the American Electronics Association showed that Colorado ranked first in the nation in the concentration of high technology workers. In the private sector, ninety-seven out of every 1,000 workers worked in a high-tech field. Colorado has 180,000 high-tech jobs. It ranks tenth in the country in total number of high-tech workers.

International Business Machines

Among the high-tech corporations in Colorado is International Business Machines (IBM). IBM's operations are in the field of information handling systems. They make data processing machines, telecommunications systems, copiers, and related supplies. IBM has plants and marketing organizations worldwide. The main IBM plant employs hundreds and is located in Colorado between Boulder and Longmont.

IBM plant, Boulder.

Hewlett-Packard Company

The Hewlett-Packard Company is a major designer and manufacturer of precision electronic equipment. Since its founding in 1939, the company has spread throughout seventy-five countries. It manufactures more than 6,440 products.

Hewlett-Packard employs 9,000 people in five cities in Colorado. It is one of the largest employers in the state. There are major divisions in Colorado Springs, Englewood, Fort Collins, Greeley, and Loveland. Many different products are designed and manufactured including voltmeters, printed circuit board testers, and desktop computers.

Storage Technology

Storage Technology Corporation has its headquarters in Louisville, Colorado. It manufactures tapes, tape drives, and tape libraries.

These are used for storing and managing data. The need for businesses to save and use data grows greater each year. Tape libraries can be used to keep track of many things. They can store and track data on a huge number of bank transactions. Or they can be used to store medical records of thousands of patients. Such systems can keep track of a warehouse full of goods.

Ball Corporation
Another large business in Colorado is Ball Corporation. Ball Corporation is one of the world's leading producers of metal and plastic packaging. They make metal and plastic containers for foods and drinks.

The Ball Corporation also owns the Ball Aerospace Systems Division that is based in Broomfield. This company is often in the news when there are articles about astronauts going up in a space shuttle. Ball's products help people to discover more about Earth and to explore the universe.

Some of the equipment that is used in U.S. space exploration has been made at the Ball aerospace plant. Ball has built 130 complex instruments and twelve spacecrafts for NASA missions. They built a space-based cooled telescope that is being used to map the universe.

Ball Aerospace Systems Division.

Oil and Gas
Natural gas production has been increasing in the Rockies. With the country's growing energy needs, some look to the Rocky Mountains as an area likely to boom. There will probably be more drilling in Colorado, Montana, and Wyoming.

The value of oil produced in Colorado in 2000 was more than $400 million. The value of natural gas produced in the state was

Eyeglasses for a Telescope

NASA's Hubble Space Telescope was built by Ball and deployed in 1990 by the crew of the Space Shuttle *Discovery*. With this telescope, scientists hoped to peer deeper into the heavens than ever before. What a disappointment when they discovered a flaw on the telescope that greatly limited Hubble's ability to properly focus light.

Instead of getting discouraged and giving up, scientists went back to work again. They came up with COSTAR (Corrective Optics Space Telescope Axial Replacement). When astronauts again went up to the telescope, they put COSTAR in place and corrected the problem. Basically, scientists put a pair of corrective eyeglasses on the telescope.

The Hubble Telescope, with its eyeglasses, sent back valuable data to scientists on Earth.

$2.35 billion. Colorado ranks tenth in the United States in oil production and sixth in gas production. There were 18,473 oil and gas wells producing in Colorado in 1999 with approximately 19,000 employees.

Wind Power and Nuclear/Gas Power

Sometimes there are energy shortages in the United States, and people are looking for alternatives to their heavy reliance on oil. One alternative is to use wind power as a source of energy. Xcel Energy's Ponnequin Wind Farm in northern Colorado uses turbines to generate wind power. Many of their current customers get all or part of their energy through wind source from Xcel Energy. Another large wind farm has been erected just twenty-three miles south of Lamar, Colorado.

The Fort St. Vrain Nuclear Power Plant, which was built in Colorado, ran into many problems. It produced little electricity, and it was shut down in 1989. The plant, thirty-five miles north of Denver, has been changed to a natural gas–fired plant. In 2001, the plant was generating enough power to meet the needs of about 700,000 customers.

Education in Colorado

Since its early pioneer beginnings, many schools have been built in Colorado. In the year 2000, Colorado had 176 school districts with about 725,000 public school students. Another 57,000 students in the state attend non-public schools.

The State Board of Education and the Colorado Department of Education give help to schools with students from pre-kindergarten through twelfth grade. The Commission on Higher Education works with colleges and universities. Colorado has fifteen public two-year community colleges. There are two local district colleges, and there are twelve public four-year colleges and universities.

Two-Year Community Colleges

Typical of the fifteen public two-year colleges are Front Range Community College and Otero Junior College. Front Range Community College has five campuses and two outreach sites. Students study arts, sciences, general studies, and applied science. Otero Junior College is on a forty-acre campus in La Junta. The college offers classes in areas such as writing, math, and chemistry. It also offers programs in farm and ranch management and in automotive technology.

Local District Colleges

Colorado Mountain College is representative of local district colleges. This two-year college offers classes at thirteen sites. Some students complete their first two years of college in this way and then transfer to a four-year college or university. Others choose programs that prepare them to go to work after two years of study.

Public Four-Year Colleges and Universities

There are a number of large and small four-year public colleges and universities in Colorado.

The University of Colorado

The first building on the campus of the University of Colorado was Old Main, finished in 1877, and it is still in use today. From that

one building, the school has grown to a 788-acre university. In 2001, there were about 27,000 students on the Boulder campus. Forty percent of all Colorado students who go to four-year colleges attend the University of Colorado. Other students come from every state and more than eighty-five foreign countries. Smaller branches of the University are in Denver and Colorado Springs. More than 20,000 people are employed by the University of Colorado, which makes it the third largest employer in the state.

Old Main, University of Colorado, Boulder.

The University of Northern Colorado

The University of Northern Colorado in Greeley is a four-year university. In 2001, the University of Northern Colorado had about 11,000 students. In addition to classes for teachers, students can study arts and sciences, business, health and human services, and performing and visual arts.

The University of Southern Colorado

The University of Southern Colorado is located on an 800-acre campus in Pueblo. In 2003, approximately 4,000 students attended in graduate and undergraduate programs. This university offers traditional bachelor of arts and sciences degrees, graduate programs, and pre-professional programs in areas such as medicine and teacher education.

Colorado State University

Colorado State University is located in Fort Collins. It began in 1870 as the agricultural college of Colorado. The main campus is located on a 404-acre site. It became known as Colorado State University in 1957. In 2000, Colorado State University had 22,556 students. These students take

Charles A. Lory Student Center, Colorado State University, Fort Collins.

classes in agriculture, science, business, engineering, liberal arts, natural resources, and veterinary medicine.

The Colorado School of Mines

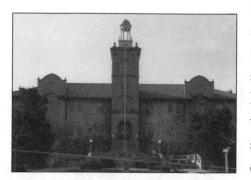

Simon Guggenheim Hall,
Colorado School of Mines.

One of the world's most famous mining schools is located in Golden. At the Colorado School of Mines, students study engineering and applied science. In the fall of 2000, the student body was made up of 2,400 undergraduates and 800 graduate students. Students earn degrees in mining, engineering, and mathematics.

United States Air Force Academy

One of the best-known schools in the state is the United States Air Force Academy. It is on an 18,000-acre site just north of Colorado Springs. The first class started in 1955 in a building at Lowry Air

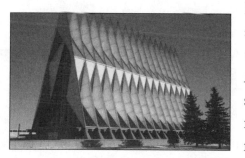

Force Base. Classes moved into the new academy building in 1958. Students who finish four years of study at the Air Force Academy earn a bachelor of science degree. They also earn a commission as second lieutenants in the regular air force.

Chapel, Air Force Academy.

Private Four-Year Colleges and Universities

The University of Denver

The University of Denver is the oldest independent university in the Rocky Mountains. This private university was started by a group of pioneers, including John Evans, in 1864. It was first called Colorado Seminary and became the University of Denver in 1880. In the year 2001, the University of Denver had about 8,700 students.

University of Denver.

It offers undergraduate programs and more than 100 master's degree programs and twenty doctoral programs. It also awards forty graduate level certificates in professional schools.

Colorado College

Colorado College is a private, four-year, coeducational liberal arts and sciences college located in Colorado Springs.

Other Agencies

Having a large state university and high-tech industries has also attracted many governmental agencies to Colorado. One of these is NIST (National Institute for Science and Technology), which is located in Boulder and houses an atomic clock that is capable of keeping time to about 30 billionths of a second per year. Another is NORAD (North American Air Defense Command) is a military organization located in Cheyenne Mountain.

NORAD: Tracking Missiles and Santa

NORAD is a military organization responsible for the aerospace defense of Canada and the United States. Once called the Continental Air Defense Command, it became NORAD in 1958. NORAD provides warning of missile and air attack. At this facility, every day of the year, twenty-four hours a day, people are on duty and constantly watching the skies.

Those at NORAD monitor man-made objects in space and detect aircraft, missiles, and space vehicles. They have a day-to-day picture of precisely what is in space and where it is located. The headquarters of NORAD is at Peterson Air Force Base in Colorado, and the control center is a short distance away at Cheyenne Mountain Air Station. The control center is 2,000 feet underground.

How did NORAD start tracking Santa? It was a simple mistake. A business in Colorado Springs ran an ad in the paper inviting children to call a hotline to talk to Santa. The newspaper misprinted the telephone number, and when the first child phoned in, his call went straight to the director of operations, Colonel Shoup, at the Continental Air Defense Command. The obliging colonel said they would check for the whereabouts of Santa's sleigh. NORAD has continued that tradition since 1958. Volunteers man the phones to answer the thousands of calls that come in, and information on Santa's sleigh is provided in six languages.

Growth in Colorado

Many cities in Colorado look carefully at any new company that wants to locate in or near it. Some companies are more welcome than others. A computer or an aerospace company does not make a lot of pollution. They hire engineers, office workers, and assembly-line workers. New companies mean new jobs. Growth means that more money will be spent in the businesses by professional people living in the towns and cities.

But growth also brings problems. Sometimes there is not enough housing. Prices of homes and rents go higher. Traffic increases. The streets and roads may not be big enough to handle all the cars when people are going to and from work. Schools and hospitals may get crowded as new people move in and need services. Downtown areas may seem too small, so shopping centers are built. Parking is scarce. Towns begin to grow out from their boundaries.

There is less open space between towns and cities. There may no longer be enough recreation facilities, and parks get crowded.

Cities try to plan ahead for growth. They decide in which areas industries can and cannot build. They have building codes and zoning laws. People do not always agree on which plan to follow. Some people welcome all new industry, while others wish that no more new people would move into the state. Most cities try to control growth in some way.

Companies want to build where they can find and keep good workers, and many businesses choose Colorado. People enjoy the beautiful Colorado mountains, rivers, and forests. They like skiing and hiking in the high, clean air. They enjoy Colorado's sunshine and the changing seasons, and they value the wide range of educational opportunities. So colorful Colorado has a bright future and seems certain to grow.

Activities for Further Exploration

1. Much has been written about beautiful Colorado and how it is a great state to visit or in which to live. Write a poem about something you really like about the state of Colorado. It might be a poem about skiing or hiking in the mountains, about enjoying a Colorado Rockies baseball game, or a taking trip to the Denver Zoo.

2. If the state in which you live were going to publish a book listing every town and city in the state, what would you like to see written about your hometown? What is special and interesting about it? Write a listing for your town in 250 words or less. While being truthful, make your town sound as attractive as possible. Share it with a friend or relative.

3. One recent sports hero from Colorado is former Broncos quarterback John Elway. You might want to read more about this famous football player. A useful resource book is *John Elway: Comeback Kid* illustrated by Doug Keith.

4. NORAD is located in Colorado. Do you know where it is and what is done there? Find out more at http://www.norad.mil. If you started placing famous sites on your map of Colorado, be sure to include NORAD.

Select Bibliography

Ayer, Eleanor H. *The Anasazi*. New York: Walker and Company, 1993.

Bird, Lady Isabella L. *Up Longs Peak in 1873 with Rocky Mountain Jim*. Olympic Valley, Calif.: Outbooks, 1977.

Bledsoe, Sara. *Colorado*. Minneapolis, Minn.: Lerner Publications, 1993.

Bonvillian, Nancy. *The Cheyennes*. Brookfield, Conn.: The Millbrook Press, 1996.

Bueler, William M. *Roof of the Rockies, A History of Mountaineering in Colorado*. Boulder, Colo.: Pruett Publishing, 1974.

Burby, Liza N. *The Pueblo Indians*. New York: Chelsea Juniors, 1994.

Coel, Margaret. *Chief Left Hand*. Norman: University of Oklahoma Press, 1987.

Corey, Steven. *Pueblo Indians*. Minneapolis, Minn.: Lerner Publications, 1996.

Doherty, Craig A. and Katherine M. *The Ute*. Vero Beach, Fla.: Rourke Publications, 1994.

Downey, Matthew T. and Fay D. Metcalf. *Colorado, Crossroads of the West*, third edition. Boulder, Colo.: Pruett Publishing, 1999.

Dutton, Dorothy and Caryl Humphries. *A Rendezvous with Colorado History*. Boise, Idaho: Sterling Ties Publication, 1999.

Hill, William E. *The Santa Fe Trail Yesterday & Today*. Caldwell, Idaho: Caxton Printers, 1992.

Hobbs, Justice Greg. *Colorado, Mother of Rivers: Water Poems*. Denver, Colo.: Colorado Foundation for Water Education, 2005.

Lockley, Martin G., Barbara J. Fillmore, and Lori Marquardt. *Dinosaur Lake: The Story of the Purgatoire Valley Dinosaur Tracksite Area*. Denver: University of Colorado at Denver, Dinosaur Trackers Research Group, 1997.

Perry, Phyllis J. *A Look at Colorado*. Boulder, Colo.: Pruett Publishing, 1986.

Savage, Jeff. *Gold Miners of the Wild West*. Berkeley Heights, N.J.: Enslow Publishers, 1995.

Wenger, Gilbert R. *The Story of Mesa Verde National Park*. Mesa Verde National Park: Mesa Verde Museum Association, 1993.

Wilcox, Rhoda Davis. *The Man on the Iron Horse*. Manitou Springs, Colo.: Martin, 2000.

Index

A **Kid's** Look at Colorado

Index

A Kid's Look at Colorado

A Kid's Look at THE WEST

Further reading from Fulcrum Publishing

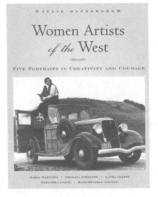

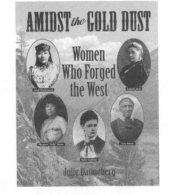

Women Artists of the West
Five Portraits
in Creativity and Courage
Julie Danneberg
Ages 8–12
ISBN 1-55591-861-1
$12.95 PB

Amidst the Gold Dust
Women Who Forged the West
Julie Danneberg
Ages 8–12
ISBN 1-55591-997-9
$12.95 PB

Women Writers of the West
Five Chroniclers
of the American Frontier
Julie Danneberg
Ages 8–12
ISBN 1-55591-464-0
$12.95 PB